What **PSYCHOLOGY**
Knows that *everyone*
should

What
Knows

ILLUSTRATED BY

Al Jaffee

PSYCHOLOGY
that *everyone*
should

BY
Daniel Goleman
Jonathan Freedman

LEWIS PUBLISHING COMPANY
Lexington, Massachusetts

Text and illustrations copyright©1981 by The Lewis Publishing Company, Inc.
First Edition

Produced in the United States of America.
Designed by Douglas Kubach.
Published by The Lewis Publishing Company, Inc., Lexington, Massachusetts 02173.
Distributed by The Stephen Greene Press, Fessenden Road at Indian Flat, Brattleboro, Vermont 05301.

LIBRARY OF CONGRESS CATALOGING IN PUBLICATION DATA

Goleman, Daniel.
  What psychology knows that everyone should.

  Includes index.
  1. Psychology. I. Freedman, Jonathan L.
II. Title.
BF121.G64   150   81-8463
ISBN 0-86616-010-8   AACR2

Contents

What **PSYCHOLOGY** Knows that *everyone* **should**

Foreword

Psychology deals with how people and other animals behave, how they think and reason, how and why they act the way they do, and why sometimes their minds do not work right. In a sense, this includes practically everything about people, every question you might be tempted to ask about how we tick. This book is a collection of some of the more important and interesting findings of modern psychology. Obviously, it is only a small sample of what psychology knows, but we think it gives a good picture of the field and also includes many of the things people are most curious about. We have avoided the most technical aspects of psychology, and have not tried to explain the complex theories or controversies. Instead, we focus on the surprising findings—those that most people would not have predicted—and the basic, important findings, which you may not find surprising but which tell us a great deal about how people function.

All of the facts and discussions in the book are based on solid research done by psychologists or other scientists. When the finding or idea is still speculative, we have indicated this, but most of the book consists of those things about which psychologists are pretty certain. We have taken the material from journal articles, books, talks at conferences, and symposia. Our goal was to write a book that showed just how fascinating psychology can be and that would answer some of the questions people have about themselves.

How We See the World

We know the world around us through our senses—vision, hearing, smell, taste, and touch. Without them we would be totally cut off. Human senses are remarkably good. We sometimes think that other animals have much better senses than we do—they can see in the dark, or hear a pin drop miles away. But actually, our eyes and ears in particular are incredibly sensitive and make us the equal of most other animals.

We take our senses so much for granted that we usually do not realize how amazingly complex they are. Psychologists and others have studied how our eyes and ears work in great detail, and psychologists in particular have concentrated on trying to understand how we take all the information gathered by our senses and organize it so that the world has some coherence, so it fits together rather than being a hodgepodge of sights and sounds. Psychologists have also studied why we are sometimes fooled by our senses, why they break down or work in such a way that we get incorrect information.

The items here avoid dealing with the great complexity of

3

our sensory system. They do not discuss the physical apparatus much, nor how the neurons and so on work. Rather, we have focused on those curious and interesting facts that tell us something about perception that we did not know before.

Oh Say Can You See (Or Hear? Taste? Smell? Feel?)

Each sense has a lowest limit for sensitivity, the weakest stimulus it can detect. These are, to wit:

Vision	A candle burning on a clear, dark night 50 kilometers away
Hearing	A watch ticking 6 meters away in a quiet room
Taste	One gram of salt diluted in 500 liters of water
Smell	A single drop of perfume spread through a three-room apartment
Touch	A bee's wing falling on your cheek from 1 centimeter

Within their range of sensitivity, our senses are exquisitely tuned for their tasks. While the ears register frequencies of sound between 20 and 20,000 cycles per second, their maximum sensitivity is between 1,000 and 4,000 cycles—the range that human speech falls in. The eyes can discriminate two lines at a distance of 50 centimeters. The skin is extremely good at discriminating, though it is more sensitive in some places than others; the back, arm, and thigh can tell the difference between two points of touch if they fall 7.0 centimeters apart, but the fingertips can discriminate between them if they are just 0.3 centimeters apart. And the tongue can tell the difference between two tastes that alternate as rapidly as five times each second.

Optical Illusions—What You See Is Anybody's Guess (or Fooling The Eyes)

Most of the time we can trust our eyes to tell us what is going on in the world, but sometimes our eyes lie to us—we see things very differently from reality. Consider the illustrations. In 1, you probably see line A as longer than line B; the same in 2; and in 3, circle A almost certainly looks smaller than circle B. Yet the lines are exactly the same length in 1 and 2, and the circles exactly the same size in 3. (Measure them yourself—these effects are so powerful, sometimes you have to use a ruler to convince yourself.)

No one knows for sure why we see these illusions. There are lots of theories, but none is entirely convincing. For the moment, we know that illusions do occur and are trying to find out why.

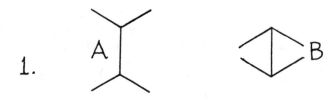

Vertical line "A" looks longer than vertical line "B", but they are actually the same length.

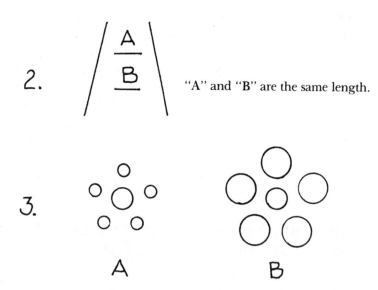

"A" and "B" are the same length.

The center circles in "A" and "B" are the same size, although "A" looks bigger.

A Door Is a Door Is a Door

When we see a man at the end of the block walking toward us, he does not seem tiny, nor does he get larger and larger as he approaches. Rather, we see him as being the same size the whole time. Yet his image on our eyes (actually our retinas) is much much smaller when he is a block away than when he is close by. This tendency to see things the same way despite changing conditions is called perceptual constancy—our perceptions stay the same. It is a crucial part of our perceptual process.

Imagine how impossible the world would be if familiar objects were constantly seeming to change in size or shape—a tiny person one minute, a full-grown one another; an insect-size toy car a block away and suddenly a full-size car bearing down on us. We would be totally bewildered. Instead, everything is serene and easy, because most objects do not change in size or shape.

Consider a door—a simple object, totally familiar. We look at a closed door and it is obviously rectangular. Then the door opens and it is still rectangular; it opens more and is still the same familiar shape. Yet if you imagine for a moment what a

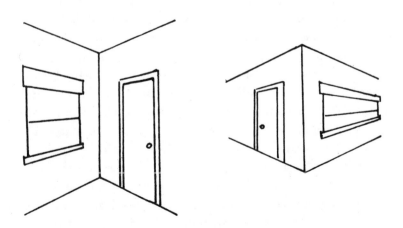

The center vertical line in each drawing is the same length.

door looks like as it opens (try looking at one in the room), you will realize that the shape you see is not a rectangle but a trapezoid. The side nearer you is larger than the one away from you, and the door itself is narrower than when it is closed. That is, these are the images that hit your eye—if you took a picture of an open door and outlined the door, you would have a trapezoid, not a rectangle. Yet we see it as a rectangle no matter what. It's a good thing—otherwise, how would it fit back in the doorway?

Those Spots before Your Eyes—And the Trees Inside

Even while sober you may have noticed spots—or wavy lines—floating before your eyes. They may seem to drift lazily to one side while your eye is still. When your eye moves, though, so do they.

Some people call these spots "floaters." Their technical name is *phosphenes.* They are caused by impurities that float in the fluids inside the eyeball. As these bits of tissue float along, they cast shadows on the retina. If the eye is looking at something that provides a background both bright and unbroken—like the sky—then the phosphenes seem to be hovering in space.

When the eye doctor shines a light in your eye during an exam, a similar effect occurs. The light shines into your retina, and you see what looks like a translucent tree with lots of branches. There's no tree, of course; it's the blood vessels in your own retina. These blood vessels are normally unseen, even though they are always present in your retina; you look right through them to see anything else. Because they're always there, the part of the brain that receives messages from your eyes ignores them. You stay unaware of them until the shining light gives them a dramatic new look, and your brain reacts differently to them.

Want to see the tree in your eye? Go into a dark room, and

shine a small flashlight beam into your eye from the side and above your head. If someone asks you what you're up to, though, we suggest you don't tell them you're trying to see the trees in your eyes. . . .

Your Blind Spot

We all share a blind spot, and we are almost never aware of it. Each eye has a spot where it registers nothing, located at that point in the back of the eyeball where the optic nerve, which runs to the brain, is attached to the retina. Although the rest of the retina has special cells that register the light that comes through the lens of the eye, our "blind spot" lacks these cells and, therefore, we have a blind spot in each eye.

We don't ordinarily notice these blind spots because we see with both eyes and each registers a slightly different part of what we look at. The overlap from each eye fills in what the blind spot of the other eye can't see.

You don't believe us—well if you want to find your blind spot here's how to do it.

Close your right eye, hold the book at arm's length, and focus on the X.
Very slowly move the book toward you. When the circle falls in your blind spot it will disappear.

To find your other blind spot, do the following.

Close your left eye, hold the book at arm's length, and focus on the circle.
Notice when the X disappears when you move the book toward you very, very slowly.

Stars in Your Eyes

Uncle Harry just can't get that damn picture right, little Georgie won't stop picking his nose, Aunt Sarah says she had her eyes closed again, and you're seeing a colored dot in the middle of whatever you look at from the popping of the latest flash bulb. Even if you close your eyes, the dot remains. The light that lingers is an afterimage, a product of how the visual system operates.

When Uncle Harry takes the picture, the flash bulb creates a "positive" afterimage and your brain cells continue to register the bright light even after the initial flash is gone.

You can also get a "negative" afterimage, so-called because the color that lingers is the opposite of the original—if red was the original the afterimage will be blue-green. The negative afterimage occurs because those cells in the eye that register the original color are very active when you stare at the color and become fatigued after a while; consequently, they respond less and less strongly. When you then look at a neutral background, your eye is exposed to light of many frequencies and colors. If the fatigued cells were responding to red previously, they now respond less strongly than the cells that register red's opposite color (blue-green in this case), which appears as an afterimage in that part of the visual field where the tired cells are.

It's a Plane

One dangerous situation in World War II had nothing to do with the Axis powers—the enemy in this case was something psychologists know as the "autokinetic effect," and it caused real problems for pilots.

If you look at a small light shining in a totally dark room, it will seem to bounce around erratically. This illusion created a dangerous situation for aircraft because pilots flying in formation at night were told to keep in position by watching the tail light of the plane ahead. The steady light on the plane ahead would, of course, move around wildly because of the autokinetic effect and the pilots would become disoriented. The simple solution: have the lights flash on and off, as has been the practice in aviation ever since.

The autokinetic effect is caused neither by small movements of the eye nor by any motion of the head—its most widely accepted explanation ties it to muscle fatigue. When the eye holds its gaze on a stationary light, the muscles that position it tire. To counteract the fatigue, the brain sends the tiring muscles an extra jolt of signals to maintain the gaze—signals that are ordinarily used to help the eye track a moving object.

Ordinarily when the brain commands the eyes to move, it automatically builds in a perception of that movement. Therefore, the extra signal the brain sends to counteract the fatigue of watching the stationary light automatically fools the brain into perceiving movement where there is none.

In the Dark? Try the Corner of Your Eye

If you come late to an afternoon matinee, you're in danger of sitting on someone's lap the first few moments after entering from a bright street. You are, in fact, temporarily blind until your eye adapts to the dark. Research shows that the eyes take longer than twenty minutes to adapt fully to the dark, though the major adjustment is in the first three or four minutes. To adapt to the dark, the eyes must switch from relying on one type of visual cell, called cones, to another, called rods. The cones give us color vision. The rods are color-blind, but are better able to see at low intensities of light. You are temporarily "blind" during the time it takes to switch from cones—which do most of the seeing when things are well lit—to rods.

The difference between rods and cones explains why you see

more clearly at night when you look at something out of the corner of your eye rather than head on. Cones, on which we rely for daytime vision, are centered in the fovea, the section of the eye on which we center an image to see it clearly. Rods are scattered around the edges of the fovea. When the rods take over vision in the dark, the cones are essentially blind, and so centering an object on the fovea makes it indistinct. But looking slightly to its side lines the object up with the dark-adapted rods. The result is a clearer image. Try it with stars some dark night.

Phi to Your Eye

We've probably all seen one of those neon signs where a series of blinking lights seems to form an arrow. The lights blink on one after the other in rapid succession; while we know the lights don't move, they seem to. This illusion, called the "phi phenomenon," is the simplest form of the effect that creates movies and television pictures.

For the phi phenomenon to fool our eye, the distance between flashes has to be small, and more important, the intervals between flashes must be less than three-quarters of a second. The faster the flashes, the better the illusion works. If the intervals are less than three-tenths of a second, we see smooth movement. If the intervals get longer, we see halting movement. If the intervals are too long, we see just a series of separate pictures. The jerky movements of actors in old-time movies were due to the small numbers of frames per minute cameras of the period allowed. Modern movie cameras flash twenty still pictures per second, and so our eye sees filmed movements as smooth.

The rapid succession of flashing pictures in TV or movies, like the flashing lights in the neon sign, mimics what happens in the visual system when an object actually does move. When the eye perceives movement, slightly different parts of the retina are stimulated in quick succession. The brain pieces together the similar images to create "stroboscopic motion," the perception of a flowing movement out of a series of stilled images.

Wy Yu Cn Rd Ths

The average college-educated person can read about three hundred words a minute. It may seem easy, but when we analyze just what this task requires, it turns out to be a rather formidable feat.

Reckoning a word at five letters, three hundred words per minute is the equivalent of twenty-five letters per second. Each letter must be distinguished from the twenty-five other letters in the English language. The eye does this by scanning properties such as roundness, linearity, and zigzaggedness. But only a learner or a very slow reader bothers to recognize each letter; instead we take in a whole word at a time. Very fast readers take in a whole line at a glance; speed readers a whole paragraph or page.

One reason we can get away with skipping letters and words is that there is roughly a 50 percent repetitiveness in language. Entire words can be skipped without the reader losing the idea (or, to put it differently, words skipped without losing idea). There is the same sort of duplication of letters within words. In English for example q is always followed by u; leaving out u after q would be no loss at all. When a word or letter *is* dropped, the reader automatically fills it in. This automatic tendency to fill in missing letters makes poofreading especially difikult.

What the Eyes Can't See and the Ears Can't Hear

Most of us know that some animals, such as dogs, bats, and dolphins, can hear high—pitched whistles that the human ear does not register. But did you know that bees see ultraviolet rainbows the human eye can't perceive? Indeed, the human eye and ear are tuned to a very tiny part of the total range of sight and sound.

The physical world is permeated by electromagnetic waves, the reverberations and oscillations caused by the myriad energy exchanges that go on constantly. Depending on their specific causes, these waves have very different and distinct rates and lengths. Very fast waves have very short lengths, whereas slow ones are quite long.

The spectrum of electromagnetic energy ranges from gamma rays at the low end to electric currents at the high end. Within that range are such waves as x rays, radar, and radio and television signals.

Electromagnetic waves are measured in "hertz," which stands for cycles per second. X rays are very fast waves, with about 10^{20} cycles per second, whereas television is a relatively slow wave, with about 10^7 cycles per second.

We can sense directly a few electromagnetic waves: the eye sees as colors are wave frequencies in the range around 10^{14} cycles per second. The human eye registers light waves that occupy a very narrow band—about one-trillionth of the total range of electromagnetic energy. But though our eye can respond to neither ultraviolet nor infrared rays, our skin can: rays in the ultraviolet range trigger skin cells to produce a pigment that makes us tan, while rays in the infrared range the skin senses as heat.

Our world would be much different if our senses were sharper than these limits. For example, if our eyes were able to detect lightwaves in the infrared range (just beyond red in the color spectrum), we might be kept awake by seeing the heat our bodies produce in the dark. More sensitive hearing would tune into the bounce of air molecules on our eardrums and the vibration of our bodies. As it is, when you stick your finger in your ear, the sounds you hear are the noises of the muscles in your arm and hand.

Why Two Ears Are Better Than One

Say you're out working in your garden, and you hear a phone ring. You're not sure if it's your own or the neighbor's. What do you do? You turn your head a bit this way and that to pin down the direction from where the ring comes.

Moving your head about helps you find the sound's source because of differences in the ways the sound reaches each of your ears. For one thing, unless the sound is coming from straight in front of you, it will reach one ear before the other. To be specific, for each centimeter of difference betweeen the source and each ear, there is a difference in time of arrival of 0.029 millisecond. This difference may seem insignificant, but the brain can actually detect a difference as tiny as a single microsecond. If a sound is coming from a source directly to the side of the head, the difference between ears in time of arrival will be a relatively lazy 0.6 millisecond.

Another cue to where that ring is coming from is the subtle distortion the head itself produces in the sound as it goes to the far ear. The head interferes with the sound, so that it is slightly more intense when it reaches the near ear than when it reaches the far ear. The brain quickly pieces together data from these cues as the head moves. Then, most likely, just as you're halfway to your door, you realize the truth: it's your neighbor's phone.

Why Foghorns Are Basso, Not Contralto

The low blare of a foghorn far in the distance is a comforting sound to many. But have you ever wondered why the sound is so low? Why don't foghorns squeal?

The advantages of a basso foghorn are that low tones bend better around corners and carry farther. If you approach a band concert in a park, you'll hear the tubas and the bass drum first, the piccolos and the clarinets as you get closer. The virtues of carrying farther and bending better, then, commend low tones to the makers of foghorns.

Hey You Kids, Turn That Music Down!

Although our ears can detect the tick of a watch 6 meters away in a quiet room (see "Oh Say Can You See . . ."), we sometimes subject them to sounds about 100 trillion times more intense.

The intensity of sounds is computed in decibels, a scale that (like the Richter scale for earthquakes) gives a reading 100 times more powerful for every 10 units. The noise of a subway train at 20 feet, for example, is about 100 decibels; the roar of a jet plane's engine at 500 feet is 110 decibels. The noise of the jet plane, though, is 100 times more intense than that of the subway train.

The following table will give you an idea of the decibel ratings for some common sounds. Note that prolonged exposure to sounds above 85 decibels will begin to cause permanent hearing loss. Among the sounds above that level: the subway, the jet, and—worst of all—a rock band at close range.

Decibels

160 —	Rocket launching
140 —	Rock band nearby
130 —	
120 —	Loud thunder/jet take-off
115 —	Rock band at normal distance
110 —	Jet plane roaring 500 feet away
100 —	Subway train at 20 feet
95 —	Very busy street corner
85 - - - - - - - - - - - - -	Permanent hearing loss if exposure prolonged
80 —	Normally busy street corner
70 —	
60 —	Normal conversation
50 —	
40 —	Background noise in a typical room
30 —	
20 —	Whisper
10 —	
0 —	Threshold for hearing: watch ticking 6 meters away in a silent room

Would You Please Stop Mumbling?

Our hearing naturally degenerates as we age. But just how fast hearing loss progresses depends on how much wear and tear our ears endure. One of the costs of civilization seems to be a high-intensity soundscape, resulting in an increased rate of hearing loss. For example, sounds as low as seventy decibels (about the level of noise on a city street) heard for sixteen hours daily can lead to hearing loss. Sounds of eighty-five decibels or more heard over long periods are almost certain to impair our hearing.

The syndrome of gradual hearing impairment is sometimes known as "boilermaker's disease," so-called because the first known cases showed up among people who riveted together metal boilers. The cause of this malady is loud noise. Short exposures cause the threshold of hearing to rise, so that sounds we hear afterward seem fainter. That's why, after we ride a motorcycle or use a power mower, our hearing is poorer than normal for an hour or two. If the sound is so intense or lasts so long that there is damage to the inner ear, the resulting hearing loss is permanent.

Boilermaker's disease is one price of technological progress. A study of thousands of schoolchildren showed that, between the sixth and twelfth grades, their hearing ability dropped markedly. The cause seemed to be the habit of listening to loud music, and general exposure to noisy people and places (such as themselves and their schoolmates). College freshmen who are habitués of rock concerts can have their hearing deteriorate to the level of an average sixty-five-year-old.

On the other hand, a study of hearing among members of a tribe in the Sudan showed that, at age sixty, they had hearing as good as or better than the average American at twenty-five. The loudest sounds they heard: their own voices singing and shouting at tribal dances.

Quiet Zone

One of the main sources of noise pollution on city streets is honking horns. A count of the auto horns heard each daytime hour at main intersections of major world cities revealed these averages:

Cairo	1,150	London	90
Paris	461	Vienna	64
New York	336	Toronto	44
Rome	153	Stockholm	25
Boston	145	Moscow	17
Tokyo	129		

The Nose Knows

Who has not been flooded with memories of an old love after smelling her perfume (or his cologne) years later? Odors have a special power to evoke the past, because of the way the olfactory system is hooked to the brain.

The nose remembers in a way that the eyes and ears do not. If you see a series of pictures, a few moments later you can probably pick out the ones you saw almost without error—but you'll have trouble doing so a few days later. The same goes for sounds. Memory for sight and memory for sounds follow similar rates of forgetting. But not odor. People presented briefly with odors forget more of them at first—their immediate recognition rate is about 70 percent. Yet those odors they do recognize stay in their memory for months, and even a full year—far longer than do pictures and sounds encountered in similar studies of memory.

One theory suggests there is a solid biological reason why smell memories are so different from others: the way the brain is built. The nose, unlike other senses, is directly connected to primitive emotional structures deep inside the brain. Nerve fibers run from the nasal passage to a portion of the brain that used to be called the rhinencephalon (from the Greek for "nose brain"), part of which is now called the limbic system. This area of the brain is intimately involved in our deepest emotions, which seems to make for stronger ties between odors and feelings. It comes as no surprise to the neuroanatomist, then, that smell memories are intense and not easily forgotten.

Why Your Cat Snubs the Candy Horses Love

Some animals such as horses love sugar. Cats disdain it. The reason is the cat's taste sensors. Cats don't hate candy—they just don't taste it.

The feline ability to taste is finely tuned for meat: a juicy portion of the right brand of catfood will set a cat purring, whereas the wrong brand will earn a disdainful meow. The cat's superior sense of differences among meats and its indifference to sweets is to its advantage: as a carnivore, the cat needs to find meat tasty. Sugar, in fact, is kitty poison, since the species lacks a certain chemical needed to make use of sucrose.

The cat's dislike of sugar illustrates one of the maxims of biology: an organism usually perceives best those parts of its environment it needs to survive. The perceptual world of a tick, for example, consists of warmth, light, and butyric acid, a product of mammal's sweat. Period. Any other sensations are irrelevant. A tick will cling to the top of a bush for days, or even years, waiting for a whiff of butyric acid. At the first whiff of sweat, the tick drops, crawls around seeking a suitably warm vein in a dark place, and gets ready to feast.

A frog, on the other hand, has special cells in its brain that respond when a small dark object moves across its line of vision—an ability that has proved fatal to many flies. Flies, in turn, hinge much of their survival on the capacity to move quickly. Their tiny nervous system gives much more space to cells that help speed and far fewer to those that take in sensory data—which explains why flies both are hard to swat and have remarkably poor taste.

What Water Tastes Like

Perrier's distinctive taste is due to its minerals, of course. But pure, distilled water, we assume has no taste at all, right? Actually it all depends—on the state of your tongue.

Water can take on each of the four taste qualities (sweet, salty, sour, and bitter). It has little to do with the water and everything to do with what has happened to the tongue. The key is adaptation, or, put more plainly, what the tongue has gotten used to. If it has gotten used to a certain taste quality (for example, salty), then it tends not to respond very strongly to that taste. Instead, it is more responsive to another taste (in this case, sour).

Water is essentially neutral, but when the tongue has adapted to one taste, then the water will seem to have a different taste. If you eat something sour, the water will taste sweet. If you eat sweets, the water will seem sour. Eating something salty also makes water seem sour, and vice versa. Cooks use the same principle when they put sugar in something that's too salty. And we all know that if we're going to have Sugar Pops with our morning orange juice, we'd better drink the orange juice first.

When Your Doctor Wants to Hold Hands

Ever have a doctor want to hold your hand during an examination? No—it's not a come on, nor is it an outpouring of sympathy from the good doc. The doctor was probably about to examine you in a ticklish area of your body and wanted to turn a tickle into a touch by confusing some signals to your brain.

If you are ticklish, you know that being touched by someone in a sensitive area will make you giggle. But when you touch yourself in the same place, you feel no tickle. The difference lies in the signals your brain receives and sends in each case. When you touch yourself, the brain both sends the signals that cause the touch and receives those that feel the touch. The brain simultaneously compares the signals coming in and going out, and that comparison renders the sensation of touch. But when someone else touches you, your brain only receives the signal but does not send one; therefore, there is no match between ingoing and outgoing signals. If the place touched is sensitive, the result may be felt as a tickle.

Doctors know this too, and use it to overcome the problem of examining ticklish patients. Their solution is to put the patient's hand on the physician's. Apparently, the similarity of movement between the patient's and the physician's hands is close enough that the patient's brain takes them to be one and the same. Because the brain is receiving signals coming in and going out, it turns the tickle into a touch.

Why Rocking Boats Make You Sick

You are lucky—and rare—if you've never gotten motion sickness from riding in a swaying car, a rocking boat, or a rolling airplane. Motion sickness is caused by the effect of certain movements on the vestibular system, our sense of balance.

Motion sickness occurs when the body accelerates or rotates. Riding elephants or camels can produce it. One theory has it that this is because unsteady movement produces a conflict between what the eye sees and the body feels, a mix-up of cues for orienting the body. But the exact physical mechanism that causes that seasick feeling is still unclear. Oddly, birds and fish can get motion sickness too.

The more you move your head, the worse your motion sickness will get. One cure for some people is to keep their head still. Others find that looking out a window or porthole will do the trick, perhaps because it makes visual cues more consistent with the body's rock and roll. Another preventive measure: stay off camels and elephants.

Why the Station Seems to Move—Not the Train

When a train starts to pull slowly out of a station, the station sometimes seems to be moving backward. Only when the train picks up speed does it seem to us that the train is moving along. This odd effect is due to how we sense movement.

We know we are accelerating primarily through two means: what we see and the movement of the fluids in the inner ear. When acceleration is slow and gradual—like a train just beginning to pick up speed—the fluids of the inner ear do not sense the movement. The eyes, meanwhile, see objects pass by the window. Until the acceleration picks up enough to affect the inner ear, the brain will interpret what the eye sees as a motionless train being passed by an accelerating landscape. As the train speeds up, though, the inner ear will detect the body's motion, and the station will stay put while the train pulls out.

When to Go Nude

What does a burnoose-clad Bedouin in the Sahara know that the sun-worshipper at Malibu does not? When to take it off, and when to put it back on. The key lies in the ways the body sheds heat.

For one thing, it's not the heat, it's the humidity. One way in which the body cools itself is through the evaporation of sweat. We get hot, we sweat, the sweat evaporates, and that cools us. When the humidity is high, evaporation is slowed down and so it is harder to keep cool. Wearing clothes also makes evaporation more difficult—on a hot, humid day, clothes can make the body as much as four degrees warmer. One study found that at 34 percent humidity, clothed men could work reasonably well in temperatures up to about 90°F, but naked men could work in temperatures as high as 120°F.

So why does the Bedouin glide over the hot desert in a burnoose? Because the rules of the game change when it is very hot and very dry. Under these conditions, evaporation is easy even with clothes on, so removing them does not help. And the clothing can cut down on the hot air that reaches the skin, thus reducing the heat. Finally, and perhaps most important, the clothing can reflect the heat (the sun's rays) just as shades keep the hot sun out of a room in the summer.

So the rule of thumb is: on a hot humid day, no clothes is best; on a hot dry day (especially if it is very hot), dress up.

How We Change: Birth to Old Age

One of the most fascinating aspects of human life is that a helpless infant who can do almost nothing eventually turns into an adult, with all of the adult's skills, abilities, knowledge, and, for that matter, problems. This process of development continues throughout life—we constantly change and develop, right through old age. This section deals with this process of development from birth to death. It tells what we know about infants and young children—their abilities, their innate reflexes, their minds, their social behavior, and so on; it also deals with old age, and the problems and changes that occur as we get older.

As you will see, this section talks about such things as what babies can see, why children get attached to their parents and vice versa, and how children's thinking differs from adult's thinking. It also discusses just how much our minds decline as we get older, and why. Later chapters deal mostly with people between childhood and old age—this one concentrates on these two crucial times of transition in our lives.

What Babies Can Do before They Learn to Do Anything

Are you at a loss when your friends proudly hand their new-born progeny to you? Newly born babies come equipped with reflexes, a repertoire of innate and automatic talents they display long before they have the muscular control needed to learn the most basic acts. If you know about infant reflexes, there are some things you can do with a newborn that will make you seem baby-wise, and perhaps even like a consummately skilled conversationalist with the six-months-and-younger crowd. Here's what you do (you can practice now if you have a baby handy):

☐ Tickle the side of a baby's mouth. He'll most likely move his head toward your finger, trying to glom on to it with his mouth and suck (try as you might to explain that your finger is neither a nipple nor a bottle). This response is the baby's "rooting" reflex. It shows up after he's about a week or two old and lasts for several months.

☐ Place a finger in her hand. She'll grab it and hold tight. Babies as young as one week can do this trick. Sometimes they'll hold so firmly that you can lift them up while they literally hang on by one hand.

☐ Hold the baby with one hand under his head, the other under his lower back. Quickly lower your hands—especially the one under his head—and stop (being careful not to jar or drop him). He'll thrust out his arms as if he were trying to hold onto someone for dear life. This Moro reflex—named after the fellow who first described it way back in 1918, Ernst Moro—springs into action whenever a baby suddenly loses support for his head. Another way to evoke the Moro empty-air-hug is to lay a baby on his back and swat the mattress so that his head jerks slightly. Like most infant reflexes, the Moro begins to wane around three months, and is gone by six.

☐ Tickle the sole of a baby's foot. She'll splay her toes out and curl them up. This reflex, known as the Babinski (which is not Russian for "baby"), is the exact opposite of what happens when you tickle an adult's sole. We curl our toes down.

☐ Hold the baby under his arms, gently lower him to the floor until his knees begin to bend, and slowly move him forward. He should take some steps, as though he were walking. Or instead of moving him forward, lightly bounce him up and down. He should straighten his legs, as if he were standing. With your guidance, babies will imitate walking and standing long before they can support their own weight or keep their balance.

☐ Put your baby tummy down in the water, being careful to support her body and keep her face out of the water so she can breathe. Most babies will start to make motions as if they were trying to swim—moving their hands as if they were taking strokes.

The walking and swimming reflexes both look as if they were early versions of adult actions. The babies seem to be trying to walk or swim long before their muscles are capable of these actions. Yet the fascinating aspect of these reflexes is that they disappear by six months. In other words, although they look like early versions of adult behavior, they do not serve this function because they are gone long before the baby starts trying to walk or swim. Just what purpose they serve or used to serve early in our history is uncertain. For now, they certainly don't do much.

Why Do We Love Them So Much?

Almost all people fall in love with their own babies. Babies may be a nuisance, keep you up all night, cry for months, bite while nursing, spit up all over you, knock things off the table— but love for children surpasses virtually all other feelings. Why does this love develop so strongly and so consistently?

One explanation puts a lot of emphasis on instinctive, built-in processes that almost guarantee that parents will love their children and vice versa. Nature cannot allow children to be born and not loved, because then the children might be neglected—if so they would be exposed to injuries and not fed enough, and they might not survive. Also, it is important for children to want to stick pretty close to their parents, because parents can't be on the lookout every second and nature doesn't want the kids wandering off and getting hurt. Thus nature has arranged that parents love their children, and the children love their parents, so that they will stay close to each other and the children will survive.

This process depends in part on the normal reactions of the child and parent. For example, most babies cry whenever they are hungry or uncomfortable. Crying sounds awful to parents, and they try to stop it. They do this by feeding (if that seems appropriate) or by picking the child up and cuddling or rocking it. Children, of course, like to be fed when they're hungry; they also love to be held. So the child stops crying. This is just great from the parent's point of view (relief, joy) and also from the kid's (I feel good now). All of this makes the parent hold the child a lot, which both child and parent happen to like. (Remember, nature could have arranged it that the child hated to be held, but then parents might not spend as much time with the child, would not stick as close, would feel rejected, and so on.)

Children Smile

Also, children smile (see "Why Do We Love Them So Much?"). They smile without having to learn—they just happen to smile. Again, it just works this way, and there is almost nothing on earth more rewarding than having a baby smile at you, especially your own baby. The baby smiles, you feel great and smile back, the baby smiles in return.

Thus the behavior of the child makes the parent love the child; and the behavior of the parent makes the child love the parent. One of the important points of all this is that it is a two-way street. Often when a parent doesn't seem to love a child enough, we tend to think there is something wrong with the parent. But it may be that there is something inherently wrong with the child— he or she doesn't behave right, has genetic mis-wiring. Just as there are parents who for one reason or another are not very loving, there seem to be babies who are not very lovable. It takes both. Fortunately, nature, by way of the genes, usually produces a very strong set of responses on both sides so that this natural loving relationship between parent and child almost always develops.

Why Some Babies Are So Fussy

Parents are well aware that their kids' temperaments seem to show up very early—some traits seem to have been there from birth. Comments like "he's always been an easy baby" or "she's always been irritable" are giveaways. These basic differences in temperament—irritable or easy—seem related to the presence at birth of high or low levels of a brain chemical called MAO (see "The Brain Is a Chemistry Set").

The role of brain chemistry in newborns' temperaments was discovered when researchers took blood samples from umbilical cords (a procedure that tests the newborn's blood, not the mother's) and analyzed it for levels of MAO. Within three days of birth they had the newborns rated on a standard test of infant behavior. They found that the high MAO infants were more irritable, more active, and harder to console.

Though there is no direct evidence as yet that MAO levels at birth prevail through a person's lifetime, there is evidence that adult temperament is related to MAO levels. Among men, low MAO levels are related to a lessened ability to handle stress well and a higher risk of mental disorder. For women, oddly, the reverse is the case: *high* levels of MAO correlate with pathology— but also with being an easy baby.

All-Day Suckers

There is one thing that babies have to do to survive, and that is suck. They don't eat with spoons, they can't drink from a glass, and it's too much trouble to feed them if you can possibly avoid it. So they generally have to do their own sucking to get any nourishment. It happens that nature has taken care of this problem remarkably well. Babies suck on almost anything that ends up in their mouth (and they put just about anything they can in their mouth). So when a nipple appears in their mouth, they suck and suck and suck. What's more, in some respects babies can suck better than adults. The trick, of course, is not only to suck but also to swallow—it doesn't do any good if all the milk spills out of the mouth. And babies can swallow about three times as fast as adults while they are sucking. Also, babies can suck and breathe at the same time, because instead of inhaling when they suck, they press the nipple against the roof of their mouth (or at least many babies do this). They are beautifully designed for many things, but perhaps most of all, they are great little suckers.

Motor Milestones

Parents always want to know if their child is normal or not. Is she an early talker? Late walker? Studies of thousands of children have determined the average course of a child's mastery of basic skills. These averages depict a general sequence through which every kid passes in more or less the same order. Remember that these are norms, and there's lots of variation: some kids are quicker, some slower. An inner clock seems to make these events happen more or less on time, and the sequence seems hard to speed up.

Here are some major milestones of motor development and the ages at which they typically occur: We've also included our own estimates of the probable damage potential as well as parental milestones for each stage:

Age	Skill	Probable Damage
1 month	Can lift chin if lying on stomach—but head sags if not supported.	Can drool on your lap.
2 months	Can hold up head when held.	Can drool anywhere on you.
3 months	Turns from side to back, but not from back to side.	Can knock your glasses off.

4 months	Stares at an object and shakes it if held in hands, but can't hold it on own.	Can start to torture the dog.
5 months	Can roll from back to side. Holds an object, but doesn't use thumb.	Can grab your earrings.

6 months	Sits up in a high chair. Moves an object from hand to hand.	Can spill anything with either hand.
7 months	Can sit up without support. Tries to crawl. Can roll from tummy to back.	Can reach things on coffee tables.

Age	Skill	Probable Damage
8 months	Stands if supported or holding on. Crawls with arms pulling self along. Can use thumb when grasping. Picks up small objects—and drops them.	Can drop ten cans of petit pois in your shopping cart.
10 months	Sits up readily. Crawls around freely.	Oh God!—the baby's mobile, and fast. Baby-proof the room.
11 months	Stands and walks if guided.	Increases destructive radius dramatically.
12 months	Says first word.	Can lurch around first floor and destroy anything while saying something.
13 months	Crawls up the stairs	Ye gads! He can reach any part of the house! Buy safety gates!
14 months	Stands freely.	Can stand in the kiddy seat of the grocery cart and reach ten cans of paté from the gourmet section.
15 months	Walks alone.	Radius of damage almost unlimited!
18 months	Can say dozens of words. Throws a ball. Runs, but falls easily. Can hold a spoon, but spills a lot.	Can curse at her grandmother, then throw something at her

(Continued)

Age	Skill	Probable Damage
24 months	Says pairs of words. Walks alone up and down stairs. Can stack two or three blocks.	Loves to turn, crumple, and destroy pages of your books.
30 months	Says simple sentences. Knows about 400 words. Jumps from a chair.	Has the verbal potential to open her own charge accounts.
36 months	Can ride a tricycle, walk on tiptoe, run smoothly, button a shirt.	Not only can he get there, but he does it fast.

The Suspicious Baby

Most babies enter a period of sudden nervousness and suspiciousness at about six to eight months. Before this babies don't seem to miss their mother when left with someone else. But by nine months they get upset and try to crawl after mommy when she leaves them, especially if they're in an unfamiliar place. This distress at separation peaks at about twelve months, then gradually lessens. Its typical sign is the toddler who clings to a parent's leg (or hides behind it) when visiting a new place or who gets edgy when a parent leaves a room.

At about the same age most infants also show a fear of strangers. Again, initially, babies don't seem to make a distinction between strangers and familiar faces. For a time they will respond positively to almost anyone—strangers as well as family—though somewhat less positively to strangers. After that they will be slightly dismayed by strangers, looking back and forth between new and familiar faces as if to compare them. Finally, they'll be downright scared of a stranger, especially if left alone with the newcomer. During this stage the most comfortable place from which to meet new people is a familiar lap. And like separation distress, fear of strangers is strongest when the baby is in a strange place.

Why these sudden outbursts of suspiciousness? Nobody knows for sure, but one theory is that they are signs of children's emerging ability to distinguish what is going on around them. The realization that there are different sorts of people and places—familiar and strange—seems to emerge at this stage of development. And that realization is, for a time, unsettling.

You Can't See Me

Ever have a kid cover his eyes and say, "You can't see me now"? Ever wonder why he thinks so?

We grownups take it for granted that children see the world as we do. But a kid's sense of how the world works is very different from an adult's. Kids have to learn to see as we do what seem to us the most obvious things.

Take what psychologist Jean Piaget calls *object permanence*. We all know that if you take an orange and put it under a napkin, it doesn't cease to exist, right? In other words, the object has permanence. Well, kids up to eighteen months don't seem to realize that the orange under the napkin still exists. If you put it under a napkin, a kid under eighteen months not only can't find it, he won't even look for it.

You can test this yourself. For example, if you have a six-month-old kid handy, hold a ball in front of her and drop it. She is likely to look for it right in front of her, where you were holding it before—not where you know it has fallen. She hasn't mastered the rudimentary lesson of object permanence. Or, if you have a ten-month-old handy, here's another test. Take an object and in plain view hide it in place A. Let the kid look for it.

Do this several times until he catches on to where you're hiding it and finds it every time. Now take the same object and, still in plain view, slowly move it out of sight to place B. When the object disappears from sight, the kid will look for it, but at point A again—not point B.

But don't bet any money on these tricks with eighteen months and older. They've learned the secret that objects exist even when they've been put somewhere else.

You Can't Fool Me!

Babies eventually learn that out of sight doesn't mean out of existence (see "You Can't See Me"). But that doesn't mean kids see the world the way grownups do. It takes several years before a kid will make the same assumptions as a grownup about how things work.

Take, for example, what Piaget calls *the conservation of quantity.* We all know that if you pour a glass of water into another glass of a different size and shape, it's still the same amount of water. The quantity is conserved, even if it looks different. But try explaining it to kids four and under—they won't believe you. For example, take a glass of milk and pour it all into a wider but shorter glass. The milk won't be as high in the second glass. A four-year-old looking at the lower level of milk will tell you that there's less milk in the second glass. Even if you pour the milk back into the first glass, he'll stick to his story: when the level of milk is lower, there's less milk.

Here's another test. Take two rows of checkers, one black, one red, both five checkers long. Ask a four-year-old which line has more checkers and she'll most likely tell you they're the same. Now bunch up one of the rows into a cluster, leaving the other row as is. Ask the same question, and she'll almost certainly tell you that the row of five has more checkers than the cluster of five.

You can explain how the milk in the two glasses and the checkers in the two rows are equal until you're blue in the face. It doesn't get through. Most kids don't catch on until they're five, or even later.

Why Kids Suck Their Thumbs

No one knows for sure, but experts offer three going theories. Take your pick.

One theory traces thumb-sucking to two infant reflexes, rooting and searching (see "What Babies Can Do before They Learn to Do Anything"). When you stroke a baby's face near her mouth, she will turn her head toward your finger and open her mouth. If she finds it, she'll latch onto your finger and begin to suck. These reflexes, of course, are most useful when you happen to be offering a nipple instead of a finger. Anyhow, if an infant happens to feel his own hand (or thumb) against his cheek, he'll latch onto that and start sucking. The theory holds that this is the beginning of the thumb-sucking habit. Indeed, during the first three months of life (when these reflexes operate), if you cover a baby's hands while he sleeps, he's much less likely to acquire the thumb-sucking habit.

Another theory holds that thumb-sucking is caused by the way the infant is fed. If the mother doesn't allow an infant enough sucking time, the infant will make it up on her own with whatever is handy—usually her thumb. From this view it follows that the way to cure thumb-sucking is to increase feeding (and sucking) time.

The third view is directly opposed to the second. It suggests that babies suck their thumbs just because the pleasure they get from it reminds them of eating. Proponents of the pleasure-from-eating theory say that the cure is in shortening feeding time, thus weakening the link between pleasure from eating and pleasure from sucking. This third view was tested against the second in an experiment where feeding time was varied. The result: the longer the feeding, the more thumb-sucking. The implications are unclear, though, since the study used rhesus monkeys instead of human babies.

By the way: once a kid starts the thumb-sucking habit and continues it beyond six or seven months, it is hard to break. Thumb-sucking is, of course, highly comforting, so kids are reluctant to give it up. Typically at around four or five a thumb-sucker will stop on his own, often because of teasing from other kids.

©Jaff

The SIDS Puzzle

An infant quietly and mysteriously dies in her sleep. These deaths, known to physicians as the "sudden infant death syndrome," or SIDS, and commonly called "crib deaths," are a medical puzzle.

In America, SIDS takes more lives in the first year than any other cause. Autopsies invariably show that there is no specific cause of death. Even so, studies have revealed some common background patterns. Infants who fall victim to SIDS are more likely to be small or premature; to have young mothers; to have had difficulties during delivery; and to seem more lethargic to their parents than did their other children.

We don't know why SIDS happens. One theory is that it may be the result of a failure in the infant's central nervous system in learning how to turn reflexes into voluntary actions. Specifically, most newborns will automatically struggle to free their breathing if something blocks it. This reflexive action, along with other reflexes, disappears starting at around two to four months after birth. During that period, infants' nervous systems must learn to voluntarily control responses (such as clearing their throats and noses) that were previously done as reflexes. The critical period when this learning begins—two to four months—is when most cases of SIDS occur. According to this theory, then, SIDS is due to an infant's nervous system failing to learn in time the rudimentary skill of keeping passages open for breathing.

If You Have Two Children, How Close Should They Be in Age?

You've decided to have two children (about the national average). The question, then, is how close together you should space them. Should they be very close (a year or two), or further apart? Conventional wisdom on this important question takes both sides. If children are close together they will be better friends, provide more companionship for each other, and generally be closer. And you get the most difficult period of childrearing out of the way all at once. On the other hand, when they are close they are competing more for their parents' limited time and so there will be more resentment and rivalry. If children are further apart, on the other hand, the older one can act as a parent substitute for the younger one (especially if the older is a girl); it is easier for the parents if they have to take care of only one infant at a time; and there will be less rivalry. Take your choice . . . except that all of this conventional wisdom (save the point of ease for the parents) seem to be wrong. Recent evidence shows that the interval between the children has little effect on how they treat each other; nor does it matter much if they are the same or different sexes, or if the older is a girl or a boy.

Children have been observed in their own homes for a great many hours. It turns out that children play together a great deal, whether they are a year apart or three years, and whether they are both boys, both girls, or one of each. Also, they are nice to each other much of the time and fight at other times, regardless of the interval between them. Children who are close together in age fight just as much as and no more than children who are far apart; and they are just as nice to each other also.

If you have two children, then, you can expect that they will play together, be companions for each other, fight some, help some, and generally be important in each other's lives. Their age and sex don't matter as much as you may have thought.

When Little Geniuses Grow Up

Folklore about precocious geniuses holds that "early ripe, early rot." The assumption about those five-year-old concert violinists or nine-year-old chess champs is that as they age they will drift into obscurity and failure. By and large, though, this is not at all the case.

The definitive study of the life course of geniuses is still in progress, after more that sixty years. Way back in post-World-War-I California, a group of Stanford psychologists sifted through IQ scores of the state's schoolchildren. Out of a quarter of a million children, they spotted 1,528 whose scores marked them in the top 1 percent of intelligence—an IQ of 135 or above on the tests they gave. These kids (now mostly in their seventies) have been interviewed and tested every five years or so ever since.

Pessimists to the contrary, these bright young kids matured into successful adults, both psychologically and professionally. As a group, they were well adjusted in school and did well. As might be expected, a very high proportion of them went on to get an advanced education, even though they hit college during the depression years. Their average income as adults was far above the national average. By midlife, many were listed in *Who's Who;* their combined output of scholarly publications, books, and patents was prodigious.

Personally, they also fared well. They had about the same number of divorces as the national norm for their age group. But they were also highly satisfied with their private and family life. And although they were better off than others of their generation, when they looked back on sources of satisfaction, money made no difference.

Discipline

How do you discipline a child to behave the way you want, but at the same time not resent or hate you and also retains some independence and initiative? This is one of the most important questions concerning parenthood, and unfortunately we do not have a final answer. But there are some hints regarding types of discipline.

Generally we can divide discipline into three general types. First we have parents who require strict conformity, who exert strong control over their children and demand unquestioning obedience. These authoritarian parents may use punishment of various kinds, but that is less important than their strong demands. In contrast are parents who allow their children to do almost anything they want, are warm, and require little obedience. They may ask their children to make the bed or something, but they do not require it. They are permissive. And then there are parents who somehow exert firm control over their children—the children do pretty much what the parent wants—but without punishment. The children understand what the parent desires and try to please the parent.

When they enter school, children from these three kinds of homes differ considerably. The children from authoritarian homes are distrustful, withdrawn, and discontent; the children from permissive homes are in between—getting along quite well, but with some problems; and the best off are those from the last category—they are self-reliant and confident, and they control themselves rather than having to be controlled by the teacher. Exactly how to accomplish this kind of disciplining is unclear—perhaps with love combined with a strong sense of what is right and what you want your children to do. What is clear is that these children seem to be better off than children of parents who are either too authoritarian or too permissive.

Girls Are Taller?

Do you remember that brief time in your life when girls were actually taller than boys of the same age? The big growth spurt for both sexes occurs around puberty—somewhere between ten and fifteen. Before this, boys are on average taller than girls. But girls reach puberty earlier, and they start their growth spurt earlier. This means that for a year or two, when they are all about eleven or twelve, girls are taller. Then the boys start reaching puberty, their growth spurt starts, and of course they are soon taller on average than the girls. All of this means that in fifth-and sixth-grade classes, you will find lots of very tall girls, a few tall boys (very early puberty), and many boys who are awfully small compared to those great big girls. Most men have trouble remembering this. . . .

The Invention of Adolescence

Adolescence as we know it—with teen-agers living at home in a prolonged dependence on their parents—is an invention of this century. In revolutionary America kids left home far earlier than they do these days. For poor families (and most were), the older a child, the more space and food he or she took up—and the greater the incentive to send the child away. One typical arrangement for boys as young as seven was to be sent to a wealthy farmer's spread as a "boy of all work." The sons of farmers themselves left home seasonally, heading for boarding school in winter and back home in summer to help on the farm. Even wealthy merchants sent their sons to sea as cabin boys before they were ten, part of a process that could culminate in a partnership in a shipping company. In eighteenth-century America, the typical pattern was of several partings and returns, beginning as early as seven, that would lead to a final break in the late teen years.

The growth of cities in the mid-nineteenth century made early partings more permanent. The demand for factory workers was frequently filled by youngsters of both sexes; the typical pattern became a rural childhood followed by an early urban career. The difficulty of travel and rigidity of work schedules made children's leavetaking for the city irrevocable. The most common pattern was for children to leave home during their early teen years, frequently for good.

A combination of factors during the nineteenth century led gradually to the predominance of the sort of adolescent years we now take for granted. For one, people had fewer children spread over fewer years; the small urban family rather than the huge rural brood became the norm. As standards of sanitation and nutrition improved, people lived longer: double the number of Americans survived to middle age in 1900 compared to 1860. The result of both these trends was that more parents lived to see their children become teen-agers. At the same time, a growing middle class no longer suffered the economic pressures that forced children out of the home, and the spread of public education gave the children a good reason to stay put. So it was, around the turn of the century, that Americans started to subscribe to the idea that adolescence was a delicate stage that required parents to shield the young from too early exposure to adult life. Parents could afford it.

Act Your Age

Americans more or less agree on the "right age" for a person to do such things as marry or go to school. This consensus determines what seems appropriate; when people deviate from these age norms, others are likely to look askance at them.

Ninety-three middle-class, middle-aged men and women were asked at what ages they though people should do things such as marry. If you want to know what to do when someone tells you to "act your age," here, according to their standards, are your answers (but, of course, other people may have different standards and they are probably changing every year).

A man should marry	between 20 and 25
A woman should marry	between 19 and 24
People should become grandparents	between 45 and 50
People should finish school and start working	between 20 and 22
People should settle on their careers	between 24 and 25
People should be at the peak of their careers	between 45 and 50
People should retire	between 60 and 65
A man accomplishes most	between 40 and 50
A woman has the most responsibilities	between 25 and 40
A woman looks her best	between 20 and 35

A person is:
"young" .... between 18 and 24
"middle-aged" .... between 40 and 50
"old" .... between 60 and 75

When Do People Marry?

The current trend is for young men and women to wait longer before marrying. The average age at first marriage for women is twenty-two, for men twenty-four. The postponement of marriage is a trend that began way back in the 1950's, when the average age at marriage was just under twenty-three for men and about twenty for women.

But—guess what? This modern trend takes us back almost a century: in 1890 the average age for women to marry was twenty-two, for men twenty-six.

The New Stay-at-Homes

Though young people look forward to moving out of their parents' home as a key step in growing up (see "The Invention of Adolescence"), more young people are staying home longer these days. In 1969, for example, census figures showed that of those over fourteen who lived at home, one in five was between twenty and twenty-nine; by 1979 that proportion had climbed to one in four.

The trend toward staying home longer reflects two general shifts in American society: people are marrying later, and money is tighter. The age of Americans at first marriage has risen steadily over the last three decades, whereas the divorce rate for those under thirty has more than tripled in the last twenty years. In addition, over the last decade the average income of those between twenty-four and thirty-four dropped by more than $700. And marriage and money have traditionally been the keys to the door for the young.

Whom We Live With

The mother-father-and-kids family unit continues to typify American households. But other arrangements are increasingly common. Latest census figures show the following:

☐ One in five households has only one person. The last decade saw this category of households increase by about two-thirds, mostly because of increases in divorces, in young people living on their own, and in the numbers of elderly able to hold on to their own homes. Women comprise two-thirds of these single households, but the rate at which men are beginning to live alone outpaces that of women. The largest increase, though, was among both men and women under thirty-five.

☐ Two percent of Americans live in someone else's household, most as boarders.

☐ Almost one and a half million households are shared by two unmarried adults—almost triple the 1970 figure of half a million. Although the number of cohabiting couples is climbing, only about 3 percent of American couples are unmarried.

☐ One in six families is headed by a woman with no husband present; most of these women are divorced. And 3 percent of families are headed by a husband with no wife. Although the number of children under eighteen fell by 10 percent over the last decade, the proportion of children in single-parent families climbed by 40 percent.

☐ Marriage, though, is alive and well. About ninety-seven million men and women are married and living with their spouse. How happily, the census bureau neglects to report.

The Divorce Boom

Does it seem to you that more people are getting divorced these days? You're absolutely right. In 1960, there were 35 divorced people per 1,000 married couples; by 1980 the figure had mushroomed to 92 per 1,000 (with about half of all marriages ending in divorce). But the boom may have peaked: in the last year or two of the seventies, the number of divorces changed little.

By the way, men are more likely to remarry after a divorce than are women. That's why there are more divorced women than divorced men—111 per 1,000 wives as against 72 per 1,000 husbands.

My Mother, My Self

There is something especially resilient about the tie between a mother and her daughter. For one thing (apart from being the basis for mother-in-law jokes), it is the strongest cross-generational connection.

The fact is that grownup daughters are much more likely to stay in day-to-day touch with a parent than are their brothers or husbands, and the parent they most often stay in touch with is mother. In one survey, for example, almost twice as many women reported having talked with their mothers within the last day as did men with their fathers. Even in a California suburb with a high rate of mobility, more than 40 percent of women said they had some daily contact, either in person or by phone, with a parent—usually their mother. It seems that, in general, the youngest daughter is the most likely of grown sisters to stay in close touch with her mother.

The strength of mother-daughter relationships shows up in other ways. For example, when young couples live in the same household with parents (and up to three-quarters of couples do at some point in their marriage), it is the wife's parents 60 percent of the time. In a study of New York City Jewish families, nine out of ten wives reported having lived with their own mother at some point since marriage; 54 percent of the wives still lived in the same building as their mother. Finally, when a parent lives with a married child, it is most often the mother who lives in her daughter's home.

The Hazards of Spinsterhood

The number of women who do not marry has doubled in the last three decades, to over twenty million.

Marriage is good for the health. Those who never marry pay a price in life expectancy: one year is subtracted from their predicted life span for every unmarried decade after twenty-five. Women who remain spinsters are more vulnerable to illness than are those who marry; they show up in disproportionately high rates among patients in general hospitals. Compared to widows, spinsters enter institutions such as mental hospitals and rest homes at a rate three times as great.

Why Your Face Ages

"After the age of thirty," Abraham Lincoln is supposed to have said, "a man is responsible for the appearance of his face." The same sentiment underlies the belief that the wrinkles and sags we develop with age are etched on our faces because of habitual expressions we make. Chronic frowns, it is said, cause forehead wrinkles; habitual smiles cause crow's-feet at the corners of the eyes.

Actually these theories are baseless. The real cause of aging wrinkles is the loss of tone in *elastin,* the rubber-band-like muscle fiber that controls facial movements. Most of the contractions of these muscles have nothing to do with emotions. However, heavy use of one set of facial muscles in preference to others can strengthen these muscles, whereas lack of use may cause them (and the part of the face they control) to sag. For this reason, facial isometrics—that is, systematic flexing of opposing groups of facial muscles—may be an effective antidote to wrinkles and sags.

Even more important factors in how our face ages seem to be nutrition, climate, and the patterns of facial muscles we inherit

in the first place. The single most effective way to keep those
wrinkles away in old age: choose your parents wisely.

But what if you inherited your wrinkles anyway—is there
anything you can do about it? Well, yes there is. There are many
"facial isometrics" that perform the same function as do other
types of isometrics. If, for example, you are worried about wrinkles in your forehead, there are three different types of exercises
you can do to discourage these wrinkles; you can raise your
eyebrows, you can pull your eyebrows down, or you can exercise
the muscle that pulls your scalp foreward.

Look at your forehead in the mirror. If you have horizontal
lines or even the hint of horizontal lines, you can work on these
by pulling your eyebrows down and by exercising the muscle
that controls your scalp. And if you have vertical lines between
your brows, the proper isometric is for you to raise your
eyebrows. Exercise—in this case moving your face around—
can help keep you looking young.

Your IQ: How It Grows and Declines

Will you always be as smart as you are now? Yes and no.

There are two sorts of intelligence, "fluid" and "crystallized"
(see "The Varieties of Intelligence"). Each increases and declines
differently. The more general, fluid type begins to fall before we
are out of our twenties. The more specific, crystallized type tends
to increase steadily throughout most of our adult life. That's
why we don't seem to grow dumber as we age: the rise in one can
compensate for the drop in the other.

One set of causes for the drop in both sorts of intelligence as we
age is purely physical. The basis for intelligence, the brain,
suffers minor damage through such common events as high
fever, blows to the head, intoxication, and exposure to pollutants like auto exhaust. Though none of these events is usually
severe enough to be noticeable, they have a cumulative and
irreversible effect on the brain's capacity. Because the brain

grows in complexity into the early twenties, these physical defi-
cits don't begin to affect intelligence until the late twenties, and
only gradually have a stronger total impact as we age. Because
the biological changes have a stronger impact on fluid than on
crystallized intelligence, fluid abilities slowly decrease as we age.

Most of us learn ways to compensate for the drop in fluid
smarts with tactics from our crystallized repertoire. Thus a wan-
ing ability to remember seven digits, as in a phone number, can
be made up for by chunking the number into clumps, like the
first three numbers and then the next four.

Because fluidity peaks in the twenties, these are typically the
years of a person's greatest creativity. For example, half the
fifty-two greatest discoveries in chemistry were made by people
not yet twenty-nine. But a person's greatest intellectual *productivity* typically occurs later, during the thirties and forties, while
crystallized faculties are still growing.

Most IQ tests mix fluid and crystallized capacities in varying
degrees, and so give different answers to the question of whether
IQ declines with age. If the tests tap fluid intelligence they'll
show a decline; if crystallized, little or no drop.

Grandparenthood:
A Growing Concern

At the turn of the century in America, far fewer children had
ongoing contact with a grandparent than is presently the case.
One reason is that, as a nation of immigrants, many new parents
had left their own parents behind in the old country. Another is
that more people live longer and so are more likely to live to have
grandchildren. Today more than two of every three people over
sixty-five have living grandchildren.

While we're at it, we may as well dispel another popular
illusion about grandparenting in the good old days. Americans
cherish the idea that, in the past, three generations of the same
family were more likely than they are today to share the same

household—that these days the generations are more alienated from each other. But the available data show that today about one in twelve households are three-generational—about as many as there were one hundred years ago.

And Not One of Them Comes to Visit Me!

A Mel Brooks record album, *The 2,000-Year-Old Man*, portrayed an ancient character who had sired more than 10,000 children in his day. Yet, he complained, "not one of them comes to visit me!"

The two-thousand-year-old man's plaint may be shared by other parents whose children have grown into adulthood. But in fact the truth doesn't seem all that bad. A survey of elderly parents found that two-thirds had seen one of their children within the last twenty-four hours. . . . Eight out of ten had seen a child within the last week.

Historical evidence suggests that modern urban life actually tends to draw families together because big cities make it economically more feasible for different branches of a family to make a living in the same urban area. This helps parents stay in touch with their grown children. More than six out of ten older people surveyed said they lived within walking distance of a daughter or son.

The Health Demographics of Aging

We're living longer than our grandparents—if we live long enough. Just about one in ten Americans is 65 or older; at the turn of the century only one in twenty-five Americans lived to sixty-five and beyond. Americans born in 1900 had a life expectancy of 47.2 years, with women predicted to outlive men by two years; by 1971 life expectancy had leapt to 71, with women outliving men by more than seven years. Despite our faith in the wonders of modern medicine, most of our greater longevity is due to such factors as better sanitation and fewer deaths in early childhood. For those born in 1900 who lived to age 65, life expectancy was twelve more years; the expected life span of those born in 1970 who reach 65 is only a bit longer—fifteen more years.

The causes of death change as we age. For those under 45, accidents and suicide are the major causes of death. But of the close to two million deaths annually of people over 45, more than two-thirds are due to heart disease, stroke, or cancer. The prevalence of heart disease and hypertension doubles in the years from 45 to 79.

A report on the state of health of the over-65 crowd also should note the following:

☐ Over half have lost all their teeth.
☐ Three-fourths of the women and half the men have vision worse than 20/40.
☐ One-fourth have impaired hearing.
☐ Only one in fifty is bedridden; three in fifty are housebound.
☐ Each year about one in four is hospitalized.
☐ About one in four will die in a nursing home.

You Know What I Miss Most?

Years ago retirement was a luxury only the wealthy could afford. At he turn of the century, only about one-third of American men over sixty-five had retired; by 1960 the proportion of over-sixty-five retirees had jumped to two-thirds, and the trend continues to this day.

Retirement, of couorse, has much to offer, on both the plus and minus side. Many of the minuses to retirement have to do with the loss of job-related status, of friendships at work, and of a feeling of meaningful labor. But do you know the single thing most retirees say they miss most? You guessed it—money.

It is also worth noting that retirement isn't as disastrous to people's health as is commonly supposed. Of course, some people who retire miss their work, their friends at the office, the excitement, and everything else connected with the job. They also feel less useful and their lives seem empty. These people do, indeed, suffer from retirement. But fortunately, they are in the minority. Many people love retirement and do just fine. They often did not love their jobs anyway, they have other interests and hobbies, they have friends around them, and their lives after retirement are as full as or fuller than before. Even for very active people, retirement is by no means a sentence of ill health—some do poorly, but most do well. But again, those who do well do so as long as they can afford to live at about the level they did before.

. . . And I Forget the Other Two

An old joke has it that one Senior Citizen says to another, "I hear there are three things that happen when people get to be our age: their memory starts to go . . . and I forget the other two."

The elderly are known for their keen memory for ancient events and their poor memory for recent ones. The evidence supports this notion. However, the gradual loss of memory by elderly people (we're not talking about the senile—for that, see "Aging and Senility") does not seem to be due to hampered recall per se. The problem seems to be faulty learning.

As people age they have more trouble learning when a task is interrupted or made more complicated—for example, by rapid presentation, brief exposure, or sheer difficulty of the material to be mastered. In other words, they may become confused by intricacies that would have given them little or no trouble in their youth. Thus they have more trouble keeping track of new facts—and they can't remember what they never learned in the first place.

As for long-term memory, it is difficult to evaluate an old-timer's powers of recall: typically there are few around to verify their accuracy. But generally it seems to decline little with age.

Our Machines: Brain and Body

Psychologists are mainly interested in how we behave and think and feel. However, all of this is to some extent dependent on our physical structure, on how the body and the brain work. Therefore, psychologists have studied the mechanisms of the body and brain in order to understand how they affect us. This section does not deal with digestion or blood pressure or muscles very much. Rather, it concerns those parts of the body that have psychological effects. Thus we discuss hormones, glands, the nervous system, and various aspects of the brain.

We should never forget that we are animals just as dogs and cats are. Even though we like to think that we are different because of our superior brains, we are still subject to the physical actions of our bodies. Drugs affect us, damage to parts of our brains can make us hungry all the time or prevent us from eating at all, and so on. Also, our physical responses sometimes reveal what is going on in our minds we sweat when we are nervous or are lying. This section only touches on the vast question of the relationship between bodily processes and psychological ones, but we have tried to describe some of the most interesting aspects of this relationship.

Temperature Kills

Although natural disasters like earthquakes, tornadoes, hurricanes, and floods can all be quite deadly, the fact is that the cold of winter claims more lives than all of them combined. A close second is heat waves.

America's seasonal death rate peaks in January or February, gradually declines toward early summer, rises and falls with the summer temperature, and then climbs steadily toward year's end. The largest number of temperature-caused fatalities are among the elderly, whose bodies have a harder time adjusting to drastic temperature changes.

The areas hardest hit by cold temperatures are those that are typically the warmest. A winter day with highs in the sixties and lows in the forties would seem balmy by Rocky Mountain standards, where people are used to cold. But the same temperatures in southern Florida double the normal death rate. When temperatures in New York City stay in the teens or below all day, the death rate climbs by about 25% over normal; in Alabama the same range of temperatures nearly doubles the death rate.

For your information, during the thirty years between 1949 and 1979, here are the figures for deaths directly traced to temperature extremes and natural disasters:

Excessive cold	10,655
Heat waves	9,325
Hurricanes, tornadoes, floods, and earthquakes	7,575

WINTER
COLLECTIBLES

SUMMER
COLLECTIBL

Jaffee

We've Got a Big Head

The human head, in terms of evolutionary time, has grown at an amazing rate. It is the one physical attribute that has changed most quickly as our species has evolved. Three million years ago, our ancestor Australopithecus had a cranial capacity (and thus brain size) of around 400 cubic centimeters, about the same as a chimp or gorilla. One million years ago, Homo Erectus (the presumed link between Australopithecus and ourselves) had over double this capacity, about 1,000 cubic centimeters. The last million years have seen Homo sapiens emerge with a skull capacity of up to 2,000 cubic centimeters. The rise in intelligence that has accompanied this increase in skull and brain size has been immense. Yet among healthy humans, there doesn't seem to be any relationship between brain size per se and intelligence.

Back in the nineteenth century, it was the vogue for researchers to try to show that geniuses had bigger-than-normal brains. Famous men's brains were removed for study after they died: such greats as Russian psychologist Ivan Pavlov, novelist Maxim Gorky, mathematician Karl Gauss, and physicist Hermann von Helmholtz ended up with pickled brains. More recently, Einstein's brain was added to the list. But no reliable difference in brain size between men of genius and those of normal intelligence has ever been found. In one nineteenth-century study, for example some of the largest and heaviest brains had belonged to a group that contained a mechanic, a laborer, thirteen common criminals—and one well-educated man. What seems to matter for intelligence are differences in the efficiency of the very small portions of the brain that control cognitive abilities. And that has nothing to do with size.

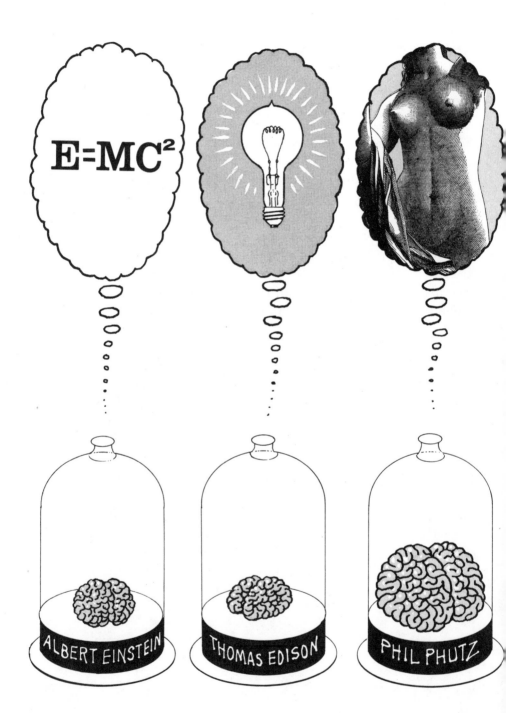

What Shape Is Your Brain In?

The heart stays stronger when it is regularly exercised; the craving for cardiovascular fitness has created a boom in jogging shoes. The same principle seems to apply to the brain; the more we use it, the fitter it becomes or stays. But *what* we use it for may have the further effect of determining which parts of the brain develop and which wither.

Brain researchers have long known that laboratory rats raised in a stimulating environment grow up smarter—and have better developed brains—than those raised in barren cages. Rats that play with rat toys benefit by having bigger brains, larger brain cells in certain areas, and more connections among brain cells. The process seems to continue into adulthood: grownup rats given the chance to explore mazes have more connections among cells than rats with no such opportunity.

The specific pattern of brain-cell connections seems to depend on a process called "synaptic pruning." A synapse is the part of a brain cell that sends and receives messages to or from another brain cell. The brain comes equipped with a huge number of possible patterns of synaptic connections. There are billions of brain cells, each of which can form connections with several hundred other brain cells. The exact patterns of these connections will define the limits of what that brain can or cannot do. But precisely which connections are made and maintained depends in large part on experience. For example, when monkeys were raised with one eye taped closed, the synaptic connections withered away in the part of the visual system that would have seen through the closed eye, and more formed to see through the open eye. In order to develop the most efficient pathways to perform a given task, then, the brain seems to "prune" some synapses while forming others. The broader a person's experience, this suggests, the greater her or his synaptic connections—and that in turn makes for a greater intellectual and behavioral capacity.

Do You Need a Brain?

Or, more exactly, How much brain do you need? The question is not facetious. Medical annals record puzzling cases where people have been found who have better-than-average IQs, have done well academically and socially, and yet, when their brains were scanned with sophisticated x-ray techniques, turned out to have large portions of their brain missing.

The most striking evidence for the dispensability of much of the brain comes from research on hydrocephalics. Victims of this condition are born with a defect that floods their brain with fluid from the spinal cord. As they grow, pressure from the spinal fluid builds up in channels in the brain cavity, causing a loss of brain matter as well as a ballooning of the skull itself that gives many hydrocephalics a huge head. Most victims of hydrocephalus are severely disabled.

When patients with hydrocephalus had their brains scanned, it was found that between 50 and 95 percent of their cranium was filled with fluid rather than brain. But even among the group with a 95 percent loss of cranial space, half had IQs in the normal range or above. One hydrocephalic, who had hardly any of the topmost layers of the brain, was an honors student in mathematics at a British university, with an IQ in the superior range.

Although neurologists are puzzled by these findings, the best explanation seems to be that the brain has a tremendous amount of spare capacity. One theory holds that many mental tasks presumed to occur in the cortex (such as logical deduction, planning, and recognizing meaningful patterns) can go on in other parts of the brain, particularly the subcortical layers beneath the cortex. Experts are mystified, though, when it comes to explaining how this might occur, since it runs counter to current neurological lore about how the brain works. Even more difficult, given the data from bright hydrocephalics, is answering the question, How much of a brain do we need?

The Brain Is a Chemistry Set

The human body has several trillion cells, all regulated and coordinated by the brain's billion of specialized cells, or neurons. Neurons "talk" by sending chemicals, called neurotransmitters, back and forth between them. Each neuron has several long protrusions that extend toward other neurons; some of these neuron branches send neurotransmitters, the others receive them. There is a tiny gap between the neuron branches, over which the neurotransmitters sail off toward the next neuron. The neurotransmitters are formed at the end of one cell branch, and, once sent, are collected on a branch of the next cell. When the neurotransmitter arrives, it changes the electrical balance of chemicals within the receiving cell. This imbalance causes that cell in turn to send off a neurotransmitter to the next cell down the line, rather like a baton being passed off in a relay race.

There are many varieties of neurons in the brain, each of which fits with a particular neurotransmitter, just as a key fits into its proper lock. No one knows for sure how many different types of neurotransmitters and their corresponding neurons there may be. One knowledgeable brain researcher estimates there may be as many as two hundred neurotransmitters, though only two dozen or so have been identified so far. Most of these are found within the brain, though peptides, a chemical abundant in the intestines, have been discovered to be a neurotransmitter when they reach the brain. Most brain researchers believe every nuance and complexity of behavior may one day be traced to the meanderings of these chemical messengers.

Here are the major brain chemicals and some of the things they do:

Acetylcholine	Controls your muscles.
Norepinephrine	Makes your heart beat faster and blood pressure rise in an emergency (and when you're in love); also flows freely during dreaming and when you're moody.

Dopamine	Helps you move and, one theory holds, makes you depressed when it's in imbalance.
Serotonin	Regulates sleep and body temperature, but that's not all: LSD works by mimicking this molecule.
Endorphins	Sometimes called "the brain's own morphine," sends messages for pain, euphoria, pupil dilation, and breathing rate. Heroin imitates this chemical in the brain, accounting for the dilated pupils that addicts hide behind their sunglasses.
Substance P	Sends a message of pain from the skin to your brain when you get a cut.
GABA (short for "gamma amino butyric acid")	Stops anywhere from 25 to 40 percent of the brain's neurons from sending off neurotransmitters. You can buy this in health-food stores.
Glutamic acid	Stimulates to activity about as many of the brain's neurons as GABA turns off and perhaps more.
Histamine	Makes you emotional. Outside the brain; an antagonist for this chemical stops your nose from running.

Brain Pollutants—I

Are our brains susceptible to pollutants? Probably. And what's worse, they are all around us—the undetectable electromagnetic fields.

We live in a sea of electromagnetic waves, particularly those that radiate from the 60-hertz electrical currents that keep our houses bright and warm. Those high-powered electric transmission lines are also potent sources of electromagnetic radiation, as are microwave ovens and microwave transmitters. In our high tech society we can't avoid exposure to high-intensity sources of electromagnetic waves.

Why should we care? It seems that exposure to the same 60-hertz range of electromagnetic fields that our houses are filled with—and that are especially strong near high-voltage transmission lines—is literally murder on the brains and bodies of laboratory mice. Three generations of mice were raised near a device that duplicated the electromagnetic field found near power transmission lines. All underwent a change in brain function, hormone production, and blood chemistry that is typical of animals under severe stress. What's more, by the third generation, the infant mortality rate was ten times higher. The most basic levels of brain function, which regulate the body's metabolism, seem to be most vulnerable to electromagnetically caused distress.

Although there is no direct evidence with humans, the results may not bode well for us either.

Brain Pollutants—II

Lead also poisons the brain. Children who eat lead-based paint, for example, are likely to suffer from plumbism, a brain disorder that can produce simple miscoordination, severe brain damage, or even death. But kids who are merely exposed to the lead that auto exhaust spews into the air are also in for trouble.

Kids who grew up in the inner city of Philadelphia were paid to bring their baby teeth to a hospital laboratory, where they also received tests of neuropsychological functioning. Baby teeth absorb lead levels that reflect the body's total exposure to the substance. Though none of the kids showed any signs of lead poisoning, analysis of their teeth revealed that most of the kids had substantial levels of lead in their bodies. When the kids' lead levels were compared with their test scores, the damage became clearer: those with normal lead levels had normal IQs, while those with the highest lead levels had IQs that averaged twenty points lower—a substantial drop. The high lead level group had trouble with simple math problems, with memory, and with such tasks as connecting dots with lines and duplicating a matchstick figure.

Lead apparently has these pernicious effects on brain function because it is one of the few substances that can breach the blood-brain barrier (see "Breaking through the Blood—Brain Barrier")—the brain cannot metabolize it well. Although we don't know precisely the impact of lead on the brain's chemical balance, it is thought to interfere with the making and sending of neurotransmitters, and to impair the nerves' ability to send impulses from the brain to the body. The only known remedy is preventive: fill it up with unleaded.

Breaking through the Blood-Brain Barrier, or Warm Milk and Cookies

The bit of health-food wisdom, "you are what you eat," is more true than most people realize. Eating certain foods can have a direct effect on the levels of neurotransmitters in your brain. And that, in turn, can have a range of psychological effects, from improving your memory, alertness, and coordination to helping you go to sleep.

The brain is protected from most chemicals in the body by the "blood-brain barrier," a ring of tightly packed cells in the brain's capillaries that filters out most compounds before they reach the brain. Until recently very few substances were known that could penetrate this barrier and so enter the brain directly through the bloodstream. Those that could included glucose, water, certain drugs, and caffeine. Now researchers have found that some foods contain chemicals that break through the blood-brain barrier, and these in turn have a direct effect on brain function. For example:

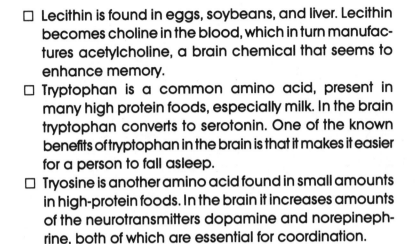

- [ ] Lecithin is found in eggs, soybeans, and liver. Lecithin becomes choline in the blood, which in turn manufactures acetylcholine, a brain chemical that seems to enhance memory.
- [ ] Tryptophan is a common amino acid, present in many high protein foods, especially milk. In the brain tryptophan converts to serotonin. One of the known benefits of tryptophan in the brain is that it makes it easier for a person to fall asleep.
- [ ] Tryosine is another amino acid found in small amounts in high-protein foods. In the brain it increases amounts of the neurotransmitters dopamine and norepinephrine, both of which are essential for coordination.

But it isn't that easy. Let's say you want to fall asleep. High-protein foods rich in tryptophan should be just the ticket, right? Not really, because they are likely to have even greater amounts of other amino acids that may get to the blood-brain barrier first, thus keeping tryptophan out or producing effects other than drowsiness.

What you really need is a good high-carbohydrate, low-protein snack like cookies to help tryptophan along by producing insulin. The insulin in turn acts to rid the blood of competing amino acids, clearing the way for tryptophan.

So where do you go for tryptophan? Where else but a warm glass of milk, just the thing to wash down those cookies at bedtime.

My, Those Needles Feel Good

You've no doubt seen pictures of people receiving acupuncture: despite dozens of needles sticking into them, they look relaxed and pleased. It seems the secret lies in brain chemistry.

One of the newly discovered brain chemicals is a type called endorphins (see "The Brain Is a Chemistry Set"). Endorphins are sometimes called "the brain's own morphine" because of the close resemblance of morphine molecules to those of endorphin. When morphine (or heroin, for that matter) enters the brain, it finds a set of brain cells ready to receive it, like a key finding the right lock. Those brain cells normally receive endorphins; the opiate molecules slip right in instead.

Endorphins, like the opiates that imitate them, have four main effects: they dull pain, produce euphoria, dilate the eyes, and slow the breath. In trying to find the mechanism in the body that could account for acupuncture's puzzling effects on pain, researchers turned to endorphins, Sure enough, several tests have seemed to verify that when acupuncture is dulling someone's pain, endorphins are at work. But exactly how those long needles stimulate those tiny molecules, no one can say for sure.

Brains versus Computers

Modern computers are absolute marvels, fantastically complex mechanisms composed of millions of parts, and capable of performing feats far beyond the wildest dreams of a mere human. On the other hand, compared to the human brain, the largest and fastest computer is still in many respects a child's toy with the mind of an idiot. In thinking about brains and computers, it is important to keep this apparent contradiction in mind.

First, consider the human brain. It is composed of about twelve billion neurons, those tiny elements that carry information and allow the brain to respond and give orders. Each of these neurons is connected and interconnected with many other neurons, sometimes as many as several hundred. Thus the complexity of the brain is staggering. Comparing it to a computer is like comparing the most elaborate watch ever made with a sundial.

Yet brains and computers each have their strengths. Computers can do certain things far faster and better than the best brain. In the first place, computers can remember little bits of information much better than we can. There is really no limit to how much they can remember, and they rarely if ever make a mistake in recollection. Have you ever tried to remember a string of numbers? Well, imagine a couple of billion numbers. Impossible for us—easy for computers. Second, computers can add, subtract, multiply, and divide those numbers with incredible speed and accuracy—hundreds of thousands or even millions of additions a second. A far cry from us slowly adding up the bill in a restaurant. During World War II, one of the early computers did a complex mathematical analysis while some fast mathematicians also worked on the same problem. The machine solved the problem in a few days; the people took a few weeks. Today's machines would probably take only a few minutes for the same problem, but people are no faster than they used to be.

That's what machines are especially good at. But they aren't so good at just those things that human brains take in their stride. For example, we are just terrific at recognizing patterns. If a hundred people write the number 4, unless some of them are really awful at writing, we usually have no difficulty telling that they are all 4s. Even the best computer can't do that—in fact, despite twenty years of work, computers can barely recognize a 4 when it is written by one person, very carefully, and the machine has been taught that person's handwriting. And when it comes to more complex patterns, like someone's face or a scene, computers are totally baffled, whereas we recognize such things almost without trying.

Also, human brains are wonderful at bringing together all sorts of information and associations in new ways. This is what we sometimes think of as creativity, but even at more ordinary levels, it is an important aspect of human thought. Trying new ways to solve problems, using old experiences to deal with something new, making up poetry, and so on—all these represent human thought at its best, and computers cannot do any of them very well.

Thus computers and brains don't really compete with each other. They have different abilities. And computers are not even remotely as smart as people—yet.

Brain Probes

Poking at the brain can have some startling effects. Researchers have touched the brain directly with a slight electrical charge, and even implanted electrodes in key brain zones to control behavior—such as stopping a bull in midcharge.

The charging bull was stopped by a neurologist who had implanted an electrode in the animal's limbic system, the part of the brain that regulates emotion. The neurologist could deliver a mild electrical charge to the bull's brain using a remote-control device. In a particularly dramatic demonstration, the neurologist got in a bull ring with an angry bull. Equipped only with a bullfighter's cape and radio set, he stood his ground while the bull charged him. Just a few feet before reaching the neurologist, the bull came to a screeching halt as the neurologist pushed a button and activated an implanted electrode.

A similar device has been used experimentally with humans. Patients who were prone to angry, uncontrollable outbursts of violence, and who did not respond to drugs or other treatment, had electrodes implanted in their brains. The results were not so clearcut, however, and a controversy ensued over whether the procedure was suitable for humans. Apart from these attempts, the technique has been abandoned with people.

Psychology labs, however, frequently house happy rats with implanted electrodes. These fortunate rats have had electrodes placed in the part of their limbic system that regulates pleasure. By pressing a lever in their cage, they can turn on the current themselves. If left to their own devices, the rats will ignore food, water, and available sexual partners, pressing the pleasure levers for hours at a time.

Finally, an entirely different sort of brain probe helped neurologists to map the functions of the human brain. By touching an electrode to the brain and stimulating it with a mild current (about as mild as the electric transmissions that normally pass between cells), the surgeon can activate cells in that part of the brain. In this way neurologists have been able to map which parts of the cortex regulate what mental functions. Often, touching the brain would activate a vivid memory for the patient, such as being at a concert. The epixodes evoked that way are so vivid, patients report, that it seems as though the event is actually taking place.

Our Disordered Brains

Current estimates of the numbers of Americans with brain-based diseases are as follows:

- ☐ 2.5 million suffer an impairment caused by stroke.
- ☐ 2 million or so have epilepsy.
- ☐ 2 million have or will have schizophrenia.
- ☐ 2 million have or will have a severe depression.
- ☐ 1.5 million have aphasia, an inability to speak or understand language.
- ☐ 1 million suffer psychosis due to neurological damage.
- ☐ Over a million elderly people suffer from senility.
- ☐ Half a million adults have Parkinson's disease.
- ☐ 200,000 are victims of multiple sclerosis.
- ☐ 32,000 suffer from brain tumors.

The Ion Fix

Ions are created whenever an atom dislodges an electron. The atom that lost the electron is a positive ion; an atom that picks up an extra electron is a negative ion. All kinds of things make ions: the sun's rays striking gases in the air, the slow release of radioactive compounds in the soil—in fact, any significant exchange of energy. The seashore, with its pounding waves, is a good ion generator, as is a storm or windy day.

Some researchers claim that as many as 25 to 30 percent of the populace have a special susceptibility to shifts in air ions. These people tend to be weather sensitive—they "feel in their bones" major shifts in weather patterns hours before they occur (and without watching the weather forecast on the 5 o'clock news). They are also more likely to be victims of moodiness, insomnia, and respiratory troubles when dry winds strike.

Some people have argued that negative ions make us feel good, whereas positive ions are downers. Negative ions are in short supply after a strong wind, in polluted cities, and in large office buildings where stale air is recirculated. Negative ions do, in fact, seem to change the balance of serotonin, a chemical that carries messages between neurons in the brain. Air high in negative ions increases the amount of serotonin available in the brain, which in turn seems to improve some people's mood and alertness. One caveat: though there are machines available that spew negative ions into the air, researchers warn that some of them generate too much ozone, an air pollutant. (We also don't really know if they work! So far, there is no good evidence that ions have any real effect on us.)

Where Headaches Come From

The pain of a headache is not in your brain, but in nerves in the walls of the blood vessels that supply your head and brain. The brain itself has no nerve endings, and so feels no pain. When you head aches, the problem is in the flow of blood.

The type of pain your headache causes depends on what is happening to your blood vessels. Anything that can change the size or shape of the vessels can make your head ache. Some common culprits:

☐ sodium nitrate, used to redden sausages
☐ monosodium glutamate, the seasoning that Chinese food is loaded with
☐ tyramine, a chemical found in red wines
☐ enzymes produced by the digestion of alcohol (that's why hangovers don't start for several hours after you've been drinking)
☐ overexertion, when the smaller vessels don't expand fast enough to meet the demands of increased blood flowing through the larger ones
☐ stuffy rooms, when lowered levels of available oxygen in the air lower oxygen in the blood, causing vessels to expand to pump more blood

The garden variety of headache, though, is caused by tension in the muscles of the face and head. A harried day or emotional crisis can make your muscles tighten and keep them tight. The overworked muscles need lots of oxygen-laden blood; when your blood flow can't keep up with their needs, the vessels expand. As they dilate, your head throbs.

The direct way to ease the pain of a headache is by shrinking swollen vessels. Warmth or massage will sometimes do the trick. So can coffee or a cigarette, since both caffeine and nicotine make vessels shrink. But the most effective pain reliever works simply by dulling the nerves' sensitivity to pain. Just as the commercials tell you, it's aspirin.

Why Migraines Are Different

Among those who suffer recurrent headaches, though, about half are victims of migraine, a different sort of beast. Besides causing excruciating pain, migraine headaches are often accompanied by nausea, blurred vision, and extreme reactivity to otherwise benign lights and sounds.

The first stage of a migraine is more like a ministroke than a headache. It begins with a small constriction in blood vessels that lead to the brain, slowing blood flow by as much as half. Since oxygen starvation in the brain also occurs in strokes, this phase is like a transient stroke. Just as in a stroke, the specific symptoms vary according to which area of the cortex is deprived of blood. If it is one area, the effect is loss of balance; if another, slurred words. If the visual center is the site of blood loss, the result is a zigzag grid of light that slowly moves across the victim's visual field.

As these symptoms pass, the pain begins. When the blood stoppage ceases, blood rushes into those same vessels, almost doubling their size. Just as in tension headaches, swollen vessels are the cause of the pain. Just relaxing can sometimes trigger a migraine attack in those prone to them. This is the cause of weekend migraines, which strike when weekday tensions abate. One sufferer from weekend migraines was Sigmund Freud.

No one knows for sure, but the brain chemical serotonin is thought to be the culprit in migraines. At any rate, though aspirin has little or no effects on migraine pain, chemical cousins of serotonin are prescribed to head off migraines. They work in the first stage but not in the second. If the attack progresses to the pain stage, then a more primitive approach sometimes works: pressing off blood flow to the swollen arteries by applying pressure in front of the ear or on the sides of the neck. This tactic, of course, has obvious risks of its own.

Who Says You Lose Brain Cells as You Age?

You've no doubt heard that our brain loses vast numbers of cells as it ages, or that every martini kills tens of thousands of brain cells. But, we're happy to report, this piece of neuromythology is overstated.

A neuroanatomist who tried to trace the source of this commonly repeated "fact" about the brain was unable to find a single well-conducted experiment that documented damaging amounts of cell loss with aging in mammals of any sort— including we humans. Indeed, when a study was done making painstaking counts of cells in the brains of rats, the only striking decline was found before the rats reached adulthood. There was only a trivial decrease in the number of cells in the rats' brains right through old age. In order to conduct this study, of course, it was necessary to kill rats of different ages and dissect their brains—one reason a similar study will likely never be done on humans. It does seem that humans lose brain cells as they age, but for most, the loss is minor and does not affect mental abilities much.

There is evidence, however, that human brains *do* lose cells under at least two conditions: with too much alcohol, or too little blood. Severe alcoholism results in a brain disorder called

Korsokoff's syndrome, where a part of the brain is literally eaten away. Social drinking, though, doesn't have anything like this pernicious effect—to do such severe damage requires years of intense practice as a skid-row alcoholic, pickling the brain in alcohol on the one hand while starving it of nutrition on the other. Too little blood flow to the brain also encourages brain cell loss. Hardening of the arteries is an extreme case of this, where parts of the brain become blood-starved and atrophy. In short, to keep your brain loaded with cells, jog before your cocktails—and have a Perrier instead.

Let Them Eat Amphetamines

A paradox in the effects of drugs on the brain is that stimulant drugs, such as amphetamines or even caffeine, calm down many hyperactive kids. Although adults who take stimulants become more active or even agitated, the effect of these drugs on hyperactive kids (who are agitated to begin with) is sometimes just the reverse.

One theory explains this paradox in terms of the brain's level of arousal. When adults feel sluggish, their brain is underaroused; taking a stimulant raises the brain's level of arousal. Hyperactive kids, the theory goes, *also* have brains that are underaroused: their frantic activity is a means of finding in the environment around them the stimulation their brain craves. Stimulant drugs slow down hyperactive kids by speeding up their brain: as their level of brain arousal climbs, they no longer need to fidget and squirm. So far, though, this is theory—we are not yet sure why amphetamines have this effect or even whether it is a good idea to give them to hyperactive children.

How to Fool Lie Detector

The lie detector is thought of as a scientific device that can detect a criminal's lie with unerring accuracy. In fact, the "lie detector" is of questionable accuracy—and can be fooled.

The lie detector is a device that measures a person's breathing patterns, blood pressure, and sweating. None of these responses is a fool proof sign of lying. However, the tester looks for irregularities that signal a rise in the person's level of arousal, a sign that the person is nervous about an answer. In theory, a guilty person will react with no emotional arousal to neutral questions, such as "Is your name Joe Jones?" But a question like, "Did you rob the First Federal Bank last week?" should make a notable difference in a guilty suspect's responses. In fact, people's responses are quite idiosyncratic; some people sigh a lot, others sweat erratically. There is no objective, sure-fire scoring method for detecting lies from the lie detector.

Because the art of lie detection is so inexact, there is the chance that a skilled suspect can conceal the truth. One strategy for doing this is to concentrate on something else—like a crack in the wall—while questions are being asked. If the suspect's concentration is strong enough, he or she should produce a "flat" pattern of responses, no answer standing out as more upsetting than any other. An alternative strategy is to make false answers to irrelevant questions. This will make it difficult for the examiner to spot emotional responses that reflect "real" lies. The "other" responses are not verbal lies but physical ones. For example, the physiological profile of pain is a twin of that for stress. Pressing a thumbtack into one's flesh while answering a question should introduce a pattern for the lie detector much like that for an upsetting lie.

Everyday Exercise
Or, The Lazy People's Guide to Weight Loss

Jogging, swimming, tennis, and other sports are good for our physical and mental well-being. We all know that. But we can't play games all day long. We've got other things to do—like sitting, talking, and sleeping. For your information, below is a list of how much exertion those other things require.

The figures are estimates, based on studies done in an exercise physiology laboratory. Figures are given in terms of the calories per pound burned off by the activity every hour—if you were to keep it up for an hour at a time. Sleeping, for example, burns off 0.4 calories per pound per hour. So if you weigh 100 pounds and sleep eight hours, you burn 320 calories. All in a night's work.

Activity	Calories per Pound per Hour
Climbing stairs	7.1
Dressing	0.9
Undressing	0.9
Driving	0.9
Gardening	1.5
Light housework	1.0
Office work	0.9
Lying down, awake	0.5
Sewing	0.8
Singing	0.8
Sitting	0.7
Sleeping	0.4
Standing	0.8
Studying	0.7
Talking	0.7
Typing	0.9
Walking at 2 mph	1.1
Walking through deep snow	4.0
Washing dishes	0.9
Washing the car	1.5
Watching TV	0.7

Those Freezing Toes

Are you one of those people who suffer from cold hands and feet when everyone else around seems warm and toasty? It all has to do with your blood flow.

How your blood flows through your body determines such things as the color of your skin and its temperature. Skin temperature—and the blood flow that controls it—can change with your state of mind. Measurements taken while people discussed their lives showed that embarrassment, depression, and anxiety lowered skin temperature, whereas both relaxation and erotic feelings raised it. Women generally have colder hands and feet than do men. One theory is that they need more blood around their organs to ensure an adequate supply during pregnancy, so they have less available for their extremities. Extremely cold hands and feet may be symptoms of Raynaud's disease; teaching people to relax—and so let more blood flow into their hands and feet—can cure it.

Blood flow is regulated mainly by a control center in the brain called the hypothalamus. The hypothalamus is continually monitoring and redirecting blood-flow patterns throughout the body to coordinate them with changing demands, such as emotional trauma or stress, or more prosaic ones such as digestion and the surrounding temperature. Since the circulatory system is basically a hydraulic pump, one of the main ways blood flow is channeled here or there is by constriction or dilation of the arteries. When you're relaxed, your arteries dilate, blood flows freely throughout your body, your skin temperature increases—and your hands and feet feel warmer. But when the arteries constrict, their shrinking diameter keeps blood from flowing freely, especially to your extremities. Your feet and hands get less blood, their temperature drops—and you feel a need for woolly socks and mittens.

Water

Your body is somewhere between 55 and 70 percent water. The water is part of the body's cells, is essential to a host of chemical reactions, and serves vital functions like cushioning the brain and keeping tissues moist.

An average-size adult male's body has roughly forty-two quarts of water in it. If he loses two quarts of water, he'll be extremely thirsty. If he loses a gallon he'll be sick. If he loses two gallons he'll probably be dead.

What All the Sweat's About

Each of us has somewhere between two and three million sweat glands. Every inch of the skin has them, but they are denser in some parts than in others: there are about 400 sweat glands per square inch on the back; about 1,300 on the forehead; and 2,500 on the palms and soles of the feet. Most function to control the temperatures, cooling our bodies by the evaporation of sweat.

We sweat all the time, although often the sweat itself is imperceptible. Way back in 1614, a patient researcher named Sanctorious Sanctorio performed a heroic series of experiments on his own sweating by sitting on a sensitive scale for hours at a time. Sanctorious concluded that he lost a pound of sweat on a normal day, a figure modern scientists have confirmed.

Sweat becomes visible as small droplets at about 88°F. On a mild day we sweat about a pint; on a hot day we may sweat as much as three quarts in an hour, or up to twelve quarts in a day. On a humid day sweat takes longer to evaporate. That may be the reason muggy days make us sluggish: moving more slowly keeps the body's temperature down, a great help when the sweat thermostat works more slowly.

The glands on the palms, soles of the feet, forehead, and underarms sweat more when we are under stress. This "emotional sweating" is what the galvanic skin response (or GSR) records to monitor a person's feelings. One theory holds that emotional sweating served a useful purpose in our evolutionary past. Sweaty hands are more sensitive, and are more resistant to abrasion—both of which would be helpful in a tight squeeze.

Still another kind of sweat is the sort that has built the deodorant industry. A special variety of sweat glands, concentrated under the arms and in the genital area, is the source of body odor. These too become more active when we're stressed. These glands start working at puberty; unlike other sweat glands, which secrete a simple salty-water liquid, these glands secrete cytoplasm, a part of cells. The amount of this sort of sweating seems to vary in accord with sexual cycles, such as changes in a woman's estrogen levels over the course of her menstrual period. One theory is that our smelly sweat served as a sexual signal—a musky come-hither. If so, the deodorant industry had better rethink its formulas.

In the Blink of an Eye

We often hear the expression "in the blink of an eye." That's pretty fast, but actually there are several kinds of blinks.

One kind of eye-blink is entirely voluntary. When you blink your eye purposely, the blink can be about as long or short as you like. A second sort of blink is reflexive: when something darts toward your eye you can't help but blink. This sort of blink is hard to estimate; its length depends in part on what sort of threat there is to your eye. If the threat is a single speck of dust, it will be short; if it is a cloud of sand blown up by the wind, the blink can be several seconds. The third kind is a periodic blink that occurs spontaneously, with no conscious intent or physical threat to the eye. People vary in how often they make periodic blinks, from about one per minute to as many as forty-six. But just for your information, this kind of blink of an eye lasts about 0.35 seconds.

Reflexive blinking has been a favorite response for classical conditioning. Innumerable studies have been done where people's reflexive eye-blinks, caused at first by a puff of air or a loud noise, were then classically conditioned to some neutral stimulus, like a word. Anesthesiologists, too, are specially interested in reflexive blinks because they are one of the last of the body's responses to disappear as a person goes under anesthesia.

While we're on the topic of eye-blinks, we should mention that nobody really knows why we bother to blink periodically. The folk wisdom is that we need to do so to keep our cornea moist. But varying amounts of moisture don't affect the rate of a person's periodic blinks, and infants don't blink at all before six months.

The Tell-Tale Eye

The eyes have been called a window on the soul. Rug merchants for centuries have watched their customers' eyes carefully as they presented their wares, to catch a change in pupil dilation. This folk wisdom is based on fact—to a degree.

The study of changes in pupil size is called "pupillometrics," a name coined by its leading proponent, a researcher named Eckhard Hess. Hess had a hunch that changes in the pupil reflected a person's emotional state. He tested his hunch by having his laboratory assistant leaf through a series of pictures of landscapes. When the assistant came to a shot of a scantily clad young lady, his eyes dilated. The science of pupillometrics was launched. Hess and his associates undertook numerous studies that seemed to show that pupil dilation signified a positive feeling, whereas contracted pupils indicated a negative one. The pupil, Hess contended, was the long-sought dependable sign of people's true feelings about what they saw, regardless of what they said. Advertising agencies, among others, were ready to

hand over millions to pupillometric soothsayers. Alas, other researchers, who took a harder look at how pupils respond, concluded that the factors influencing pupil changes ranged from people's attitudes to slight differences in light and dark in what is looked at. The changes were too unreliable to reveal simple liking or disliking. Pupillometrics floundered.

The main job of the pupil is to regulate how much light enters the eye. If there is little light, the pupil dilates to let more in; if the light is bright, the pupil contracts. This fact may account for the common belief that one of the effects of marijuana is to dilate the eye. Systematic research has found that marijuana does not in itself dilate the pupil. Rather, marijuana and dilated pupils seem to go together because most people choose to smoke pot in dimly lit rooms.

Are you Right-Eyed or Left-Eyed?

Just as we're right-handed or left-handed, one eye is more dominant than the other. To find which is your dominant eye, try these three easy steps:

☐ With your arm outstretched, point to a distant object.
☐ Alternating eyes, close one eye while keeping the other open. Notice that your finger seems to shift off-target.
☐ Close your right eye. If your finger seems to stay on target, you are left-eyed. If your finger shifts off-target, you are right-eyed.

One or the other eye is dominant in the sense that it makes a stronger contribution to how your brain interprets what you see. Because the right eye and left eye are positioned differently, each of them sees a slightly different perspective. To keep things straight, the brain has to filter out conflicting reports from one eye and take the visual perspective of the other. That's why the finger will stay on-target when your dominant eye is open.

How We Think and Learn

More than any other animal, humans are able to learn and to think. We begin learning virtually at birth and never stop. Practically everything that makes us civilized, social beings is learned—from how to tie our shoe laces, to reading, to playing the piano; from language to morality to politics. Therefore, understanding how we learn, the principles that control learning, and how we remember what we have learned is absolutely basic.

In addition, we use our minds, we think, in ways far beyond the powers of other animals. We solve problems, make up poems, memorize endless amounts of information, and are able to use this information in new and creative ways.

Psychologists have spent a great deal of time studying these issues. This section describes some of the things they have learned and that might be useful in improving and understanding your ability to learn and to remember.

What's Your Channel Capacity Today?

We see and hear an immense amount of the world around us each second. But of what we take in, we pay attention to and comprehend only a small fraction. The limit to how much information we can focus on and understand is called "channel capacity."

Our channel capacity for speech is about six words per second; for pictures it is also about six per second. Beyond that rate, we are bewildered by what we see or hear: we can't process it quickly enough for it to sink in.

For example, each image our eye takes in registers briefly, for about a second (see "Just a Second"). If we look at one thing and then immediately at another, the second image will block out the first so we won't fully register or remember it. It takes a moment or two to notice and understand a sign; if another one confronts us immediately, we won't be as likely to register the first. That's why it makes sense to have traffic signs posted in isolation from other visual clutter, as they typically are. That gives us time to notice, register, and respond, which reduces the likelihood of having to notice yet another visual signal: flashing red lights in the rear-view mirror.

How Unique

A maxim of the advertising world is that a product must be able to make a unique claim, something that will set it apart from the competition in buyers' minds. Advertisers don't have to worry, though—people often seem to see uniqueness where none has explicitly been claimed.

For example, some years ago, Schlitz beer used the slogan "washed with live steam" in its ads. The fact behind the slogan was that the brewery used steam to wash beer bottles before they were filled, standard practice in the industry. Though the ad didn't state outright that "washing with live steam" was unique, people assumed so—much to the advantage of the folks at Schlitz.

People not only make inferences from ads, they also remember what they infer as fact. In one study people were presented with a series of mock commercials. In an ad for Listerine, there was the explicit disclaimer that nothing "can make a child cold-proof." The ad went on to say, "Listerine can't promise to keep him cold-free, but it may help him fight off colds." It then suggested having a child gargle twice daily with Listerine, eat well, and get plenty of sleep, and concluded that "there's a good chance he'll have fewer colds." After hearing this and other commercials, people were tested on the claims made for the products. Despite the explicit disclaimers, every one of them believed that gargling with Listerine would help prevent colds.

Accentuate the Affirmative

Sometimes it's hard to follow instructions, whether you're piecing together a kid's "easy assembly" toy or following directions in a fire drill. One simple principle that makes people more likely to understand instructions is: don't use negatives.

For example, airline passengers waiting to board a flight were asked to help out in an experiment. They were given one of two sets of instructions for an in-flight emergency. One set was couched in negatives ("Do not leave cigarettes lighted . . ."), the other in the affirmative ("Extinguish cigarettes . . ."). When they were then asked to remember what they had been told, those who had heard the affirmative instructions did much better than those who had heard the negative. These results confirm other studies showing that people learn better when instructions are couched in affirmative language.

In short, then, negate the negative and accentuate the affirmative.

Why Does Looking at a Lemon Make Your Lips Pucker?

In the early days of this century, Pavlov, a Russian scientist, discovered one of the basic truths of psychology. Pavlov had been giving dogs food and measuring how much they salivated. One day he noticed that the dogs began salivating even before they got the food—they salivated at the sight of the food, and sometimes as soon as Pavlov (or whoever was feeding the dogs) entered the room. So Pavlov tried some research to see how far this would go. He sounded a bell just before feeding the dogs. After a while, the dogs began to salivate whenever the bell was sounded. And the same thing happened when the food was preceded regularly by anything—tones, bells, people coming into the room, whatever. Pavlov had discovered what is called classical conditioning.

Almost any automatic response we or other animals make can be subject to classical conditioning. By automatic we mean those things that we cannot control deliberately, like salivating when food is in our mouths, jumping at a loud noise, puckering our lips when we bite into a lemon, and lots of physiological responses like sweating. Whenever the thing that usually produces this response (for example, the food that produces salivation) is regularly preceded by some other stimulus (a bell, the sight of a lemon, and so on) we tend to develop classical conditioning to that stimulus and it will produce the response by itself.

One common example of this is our response to the sight of certain people. If someone frightens us by being nasty or attacking us, we respond with fear (tightening of the stomach, sweating, and so on). If someone does this often enough, we may respond with fear just at the sight of the person. The person no longer has to do anything to frighten us—merely appearing causes us to experience a classically conditioned response of fear. This can even extend to particular words, songs, or pictures that carry with them experiences related to fear or some other automatic response.

Classical conditioning can be a particularly effective means of teaching children, dogs, or other animals under certain circumstances. For example, a child who touches a hot stove and is burned will develop a conditioned fear of stoves that will prevent him or her from touching another stove (though then the child has to be taught that it is only hot stoves that are dangerous—we don't want children to grow up to be adults who never cook). Similarly, people often learn not to eat particular foods if they get sick after eating them—the food comes to produce a "sick" response and so is avoided. Although people do not generally respond unthinkingly to the world (they are, after all, thinking, reasoning animals), classical conditioning is a powerful technique for learning.

Making Coyotes Shy

Sheep ranchers have long been plagued by coyotes that prey on their herds. Classical conditioning now offers them a way to control these predators: teach them a distaste for sheep.

The technique was developed by some psychologists who sprinkled lithium chloride, an odorless chemical with a horrid taste, on cuts of lamb that they left for coyotes to sample. When the coyotes ate the chemically spiked lamb, they became very sick. After that, the psychologists paraded some live sheep by the coyotes. The once-predatory coyotes not only failed to attack the sheep but were actually afraid of them.

A similar thing happens to humans, in what's known as the "sauce bearnaise effect." Say you have a delicious meal, but afterward you come down with a flu that makes you sick to your stomach. The nausea can become associated with the most distinctive flavor at your last meal. Thereafter you'll have a lasting aversion to that food. You'll always have to say, "Waiter, please hold the sauce béarnaise."

Operantly Yours

B. F. Skinner's theory of operant conditioning is basically simple—you take an action that results in a reward (a kindergartner gets a star for good behavior), you learn to repeat that action (the kindergartner continues to behave well in class), and you create a behavior pattern that is desirable for whatever reason.

But simple as this process seems, it can be used to teach almost anything you or your child or a pigeon is capable of doing. Pigeons have been taught to play Ping-Pong and even to guide missiles to targets for military purposes; dogs have been taught to behave in the house and to perform an incredible variety of tricks; bears play football and dance.

Of course the most important applications are to human learning. Most of what we learn as children is based in part on operant learning—we are rewarded for not wetting our pants (mommy smiles), for making our beds, for eating with forks rather than hands. All through life we learn to do things that lead to rewards and to avoid things that lead to punishments. Some specific applications of these principles include teaching mentally ill patients to act less crazy, helping people who are afraid of snakes or planes to be less afraid, curing alcoholism (or at least helping an alcoholic not to drink), and so on. The methods are so powerful that Skinner claimed that a new society could be built on them (his *Walden Two*); most psychologists, however, wouldn't go that far, especially since they don't know who they would trust to organize the place.

A Chip a Day Keeps the Wolf Away

A psychologist put some chimps to work for poker chips, by allowing the chimps to exchange the poker chips for a snack. He began by giving them grapes from a vending machine. Then he gave grapes only when they put a poker chip in the machine's coin slot. Once this pattern was established, the chimps were "paid" chips only after they had completed a task, such as lifting weights.

How did the chimps react to being paid? Well, just about the way human would. They would crowd around the machine to get grapes for chips.

Some chimps put in long hours to earn huge amounts of chips—far more than they could possibly use by themselves. These chimps would run their fingers through the chip pile and play with them, just about like Uncle Scrooge.

These poker chips are called "secondary" reinforcers. The chimps learned through experience to associate a poker chip with a more direct pleasure—a grape, in this case.

Secondary reinforcers are very important to humans from infancy on—infants, for example, learn that the sight of mother's face is accompanied by pleasures such as food, comfort, and warmth. Obviously, money is the best secondary reinforcer. In and of itself, money, especially paper currency, is almost worthless. Its main attraction is in what it can be exchanged for.

The Right Tool for the Job

One view of human evolution holds that the human ability to use tools gave us a strong competitive edge in the course of becoming Homo sapiens. Indeed, some have seen our ability as toolmakers as setting us apart from all other species. But careful observations of other species in the wild have revealed some talented tool users. For example:

☐ One genus of wasp pounds shut its nest entrance using a tiny pebble held in its mandibles.
☐ Ant lions knock their prey into their pits by tossing sand
with their heads.
☐ The archer fish knocks insects and spiders into the
water by spitting drops of water at them, then catches
them in its mouth.
☐ An Australian hawk bombs eggs in other birds' nests
with rocks and dirt clods, swooping down to feast on
the direct hits.
☐ The back cockatoo holds nuts firmly in its beak by
wrapping them in a leaf while cracking them—a ploy
akin to our holding a tight lid in a towel to strengthen
our grip when opening a jar.
☐ The sea otter floats on its back and puts shells or rocks
on its tummy, using them to pound open shellfish for its
lunch.

But the all-time animal prize for tool use undoubtedly goes to
chimpanzees. Jane Goodall's reports on her chimpanzee pals in
the Gombe Stream Park describe a number of clever ploys:

☐ The chimps used saplings as whips and sticks as clubs,
both in play and in fighting—for example, while attacking a leopard.
☐ They throw rocks at each other and to ward off other
species, such as baboons and humans. Their aim is
pretty good, but according to Goodall, their pitching
arm is weak: the rocks fall short if their target is more
than a few yards distant.

I Was Educated in Your Country, at UCRA

How many sounds make a language? In India, speakers of
Devanagari build their words from forty-eight basic sounds.
English uses forty-five. The Hawaiians use but twelve.

Called phonemes, the basic sounds of a tongue vary from language to language. Phonemes are the sounds that a speaker of a given language recognizes as signaling a difference in meaning. Phonemes are not the same as the letters of the alphabet. For example, there are just twenty-six letters in English, but forty-five or so phonemes. Many letters have several different sounds, while others sound alike (for example, *k* and *c* in *could*) and so represent the same phoneme. Other phonemes are compounds like *th*. Because different languages have different phonemes, one of the problems language students run into is mastering a phoneme that doesn't exist in their native tongue. The Japanese, for example, have a sound like both the English *l* and *r*, which poses a problem when they have to say *little, liver,* or *lollipop.* The guttural *ach* in German, the rolling Spanish *n,* or the rolled *r* in French present the same dilemma for English speakers. And the click sound in Bantu—described as similar to the sound you would make if you swallowed a lifesaver whole, making a small air hole that popped—is impossible for just about everybody except the Kung Bushmen, who have the same phoneme in their language.

The crucial point about phonemes is that they can be combined into an almost infinite number of words. No matter how few phonemes a language has, or how many, they can be made into more than enough words to say anything humans have ever thought of saying. Hawaiians, with just twelve phonemes, communicate just as well as Americans do with forty-five and some other languages do with over seventy.

Se Habla Rhesus Aqui

When a rhesus monkey says:	It sounds like:	And is uttered when:
Roar	a long, loud noise	a confident rhesus threatens an inferior
Pant-threat	a roar divided into "syllables"	a less confident rhesus wants some help in attacking another
Bark	a dog's bark	a threatening rhesus isn't aggressive enough to attack
Growl	a quiet, shrill bark broken into short units	a rhesus is mildly alarmed
Geckering screech	a series of abrupt up-and-down pitch changes	a rhesus is responding to a threat
Scream	a short screech with no rise and fall	a rhesus has lost a fight and is being bitten
Squeak	very high-pitched, short sound	an exhausted and defeated rhesus is giving a post-fight report

Now that you've mastered the vocabulary of a rhesus monkey, does that mean you can list "rhesus" along with French and German when you're asked what languages you know?

Sorry. Rhesus calls each have exactly one meaning and one situation where they're used. All animals have a similar set of signals they use to communicate with each other. And like the rhesus, what they say and when they say it is utterly predictable. Granted that some species have ingenious modes of getting their message across. Bees dance to let their fellow hive mates know about the latest sensational pollenating spa. Whales make ethereal bellows and squeals that carry for miles. Dolphins whistle to get their point across (no mean trick—try it next time *you're* underwater).

But while animals can get through to each other, as far as we know only humans develop language in the sense we usually mean it: combining utterances to mean something new. There's no rhesus grammar, let alone rhesus poetry. And a rhesus makes a boring conversational partner.

It's on the Tip of Your Tongue

Quick, tell me the name of:

☐ the instrument navigators use to get their bearings from the stars
☐ the waxy stuff used in perfumes that comes from sperm whales
☐ the boats used in Chinese harbors
☐ patronage given to relatives rather than on the basis of merit

More than likely you're still searching your memory for one or more of these words. You may feel the names you're having trouble with are right there, on the tip of your tongue.

These very words were among those used in a study of the tip-of-the-tongue effect, when we're aware we know the word, but just can't recall it. People in this study were often able to remember the first letter and even the last letter of the word; often they knew how many syllables it had. But they couldn't for the life of them get the word itself.

The tip-of-the-tongue effect occurs because of the way in which we store information. We not only store a word itself, but we also store many different aspects of the word such as the number of syllables, the pronunciation, and the appearance of the letters. Therefore, while we may remember the number of syllables, we might not be able to remember the word itself, or its meaning.

Oh yes, the answers. Sextant, ambergris, sampan, and finally . . . . umm . . . it starts with "n" . . . don't tell me. . . .

Superstitious Pigeons and Pros

What do some pigeons and professional athletes have in common? Superstitious rituals.

B. F. Skinner discovered why while observing pigeons in his experiments. When Skinner's pigeons were about to be fed, they would perform odd rituals like little dances or particular patterns of pecking; they acted as though the ritual caused the food to appear. The ritualistic pigeons, Skinner surmised, had developed the animal equivalent of superstitions. All it took was a few accidental connections between an activity and a desirable outcome. Two hops, a few pecks, and voila: birdseed. The ritual, once learned, survived despite all the times its magic failed to work. Such is the power of intermittent reinforcement (see "When Inconsistency Is the Best Policy).

The same sort of ritual is seen in bowlers who twist and turn after they release the ball as though their contortions continue to control it. The pro golfer who always wears black during a tournament, or the hockey player who avoids having hockey sticks crossed in the dressing room before a game have more than they might ever guess in common with Skinner's superstitious pigeons.

Learning to be Helpless

Ever felt that nothing you did mattered, that you may as well just give up trying? A dramatic experiment performed on some sad dogs is instructive in terms of understanding just how that feeling of helplessness is learned.

A dog is put into a large compartment where it receives painful electric shocks. Wisely, the dog jumps over a wall to the safety of a compartment where it gets no shocks. Another dog is put in the same compartment, gets shocked, and simply cowers there, whimpering. The difference? The second dog was a victim of learned helplessness.

The resigned dog had been trained in a harness that made it unable to escape electric shocks. Because nothing the dog did helped it escape the shocks, it learned that escape was hopeless. The dog gave up trying. Later, when the dog was taken out of the harness and given the chance to learn how to escape the shocks, it could not. Even when its trainers picked it up and dragged it over the wall to escape the shock, the dog was unable to repeat this simple escape route on its own. It had learned to be helpless.

Learned helplessness probably occurs in humans also as well: helplessness and hopelessness may be at the heart of one of the most widespread of human problems, depression. The depressed dogs, though, may show humans one way out of their misery. The dogs' helplessness disappeared when they were given a means of reducing the shocks while in their harnesses, by pressing a panel. Exerting some significant control over their control lifted their spirits and allowed them to learn how to escape. The lesson for the depressed? Do something that makes a difference.

When Inconsistency Is the Best Policy

Let's say you want to train your kid to make his bed every morning. You decide to use an obvious technique: reward him for doing it. Contrary to what you might expect, the best way to reward him would be intermittently rather than every time he does it.

The reason is that rewards work well—as long as they last. But you don't want to have to give your child a cookie, nickel, or hug each time he makes his bed for the rest of his life. So the best strategy is to reward him occasionally for bedmaking. The kid will acquire the habit less quickly than if you reward him every time, but the payoff comes when you stop giving the reward altogether. If he's been rewarded every time, he'll stop soon after the rewards do. But if he's gotten used to making his bed and not getting a goody each time, then the habit will hang on long after the rewards stop.

Gambling casinos make use of the same principle. Winning at slot machines, for example, is a powerful reward: bells ring, lights flash, and coins roll down the chute. The player may have put in twenty quarters and gotten back only ten, but she feels great. Slot machines are most effective when they give just enough occasional wins to keep interest high—and when the wins are small enough to keep the house profit high, too.

Why Punishment Backfires

We all do it, whether as teachers, parents, friends, spouses, or bosses. Somebody steps out of line, our temper flares, and we do what we can to punish the offender. But whatever the nature of the punishment, it's more useful in venting our own anger than in reducing the probability of the same misbehavior being repeated. In fact, punishment can be worse than ineffective—it may permanently damage a relationship.

One reason punishment backfires is because it is often tied to strong negative emotions, such as anger on the part of the punisher, or fear in the one being punished. What is often learned in this situation is anger and resentment toward the one giving the punishment. Further, punishment can teach the wrongdoer to be more careful when misbehaving rather than to do no wrong. The lesson of punishment may be simply whom to be careful around. The moral learned is not "don't do it again," but rather, "be more careful."

Learning theorists suggest that to avoid these drawbacks of punishment, we should reward good behavior along with trouncing the bad. Punishment is best reserved for extremes, for example, when behavior is dangerous. If it is not used in anger, it will be less likely to produce anger in return and will probably be more effective. Both punishment and reward have their place. Punishment is best for teaching people not to do something; reward is best for getting them to do it.

Just a Second

We perceive vast amounts of information about the world around us; our moment-to-moment experience is a medley of sights, sounds, smells, tastes, and touches. Yet we hardly seem to notice or recall most of this vast array of sensory input. The reason? We forget most of what we experience within a second of perceiving it.

This shortest of memories, called "sensory memory," disposes quickly of the vast amounts of information that impinges on our senses every moment, whether we're driving down a freeway or quietly reading a book. We seem to hold on to those parts of our momentary experience that are particularly novel or have some meaning or importance to us. The rest our mind takes just a second to note—and discard.

I Recognize the Face, But I Can't Recall the Name

How often has this happened to you? You're at a party and see someone whose face you recognize—but for the life of you, you can't remember the name. Or worse, you see an old friend whose face you remember but whose name you don't—and you have to introduce him to someone you're with.

Don't worry: the experience is common. The reason is that there are independent memory systems for visual images and verbal facts—for example, one for faces and one for the names that go with them. While the two often work together, they don't always. And when they don't the results can be embarrassing.

(Memory) Transfer, Please

Let's say you've just met an attractive potential date, learned his (or her) phone number, and want to be sure to remember it.

You start to repeat it to yourself. Does simply repeating it ensure that you'll be able to recall it a day, month, or year later? Not necessarily. In fact, you may not remember it past the time it takes to dial it.

We often hold information in our short-term memory by keeping our mind focused on it—for example, by repeating the phone number. But studies have found that simply repeating a word or number does not always improve by much our likelihood of recalling it.

To be more sure something will land securely in long-term memory, elaboration is more helpful than repetition. If you mull over why something is important, or make meaningful connections to what you're trying to remember, more of it will stick. Every time you thought of that phone number, for example, you could recall also what you found attractive about that person, what you hoped might happen on a date, and so on.

Or, you could just write it down in your address book.

The Magic Number Seven, Plus or Minus Two

Suppose someone is naming a list of items for you to pick up at the store. You don't have a pencil and paper, so you're trying to remember them. If the person says, "garbage bags and toothpaste," it's easy. But if the person says, "garbage bags, toothpaste, mayonnaise, detergent, salami, shoe polish, noodles, lettuce, yeast, carbon paper, fertilizer, and bagels," it's much harder. In fact, if you hear a list just once, and don't study it or go over it in your mind, you will probably be able to remember about seven things. This has been called the magic number seven because it is the average number of items people can remember, though the range is from five to nine (some people have good memories of this kind, others not so good).

Although we can remember only about seven items, that's no

reason to limit our memories to seven pieces of information. The trick is to combine bits of information into one item, because, strangely enough, we can remember seven little tiny items or seven great big items chock full of information just about as easily. Combining small bits into a larger one is called chunking—producing a single chunk of information rather than several isolated ones.

Consider this list of letters: ehrseaackiruens. How many can you remember after looking at the list for a moment? Probably about seven, as we've said. Now consider the same list of letters combined in to larger units: chunks are easier. Those letters can be made to spell these three simple words, and not it is a cinch to remember the three words. The same principle applies when you are trying to remember any information—combining it into meaningful units will improve memory.

Why You Forget the Middle Digits in Phone Numbers

Let's see. The number was 743-8834. No, 743-7734. The phone number you thought you knew by heart just won't come back to you. Maybe it was 742-7334. Each time you dial it, it's a wrong number. Finally you give up, dig out your phone book, and look it up: 743-6334.

The odds are that the errors you made in recalling the number were in the middle digits, not those at the beginning or end of the number. This tendency to forget items in the middle of a list is called the "serial position effect." If you try to memorize any list—numbers, words, anthing—you will remember the items at the beginning and end of the list better than those in the middle.

The reason for this is that when you learn the first one or two items, that's all you have to learn. But by the time the third and fourth items come along, you are already trying to remember the first two, so the next two get confused with the first two. And in a long list, the more items there are, the more likely they are to be confused with each other. Yet the first few were firmly fixed in your mind, so they stay even though the others get mixed up. This is called interference—the items interfere with each other. At the end of the list, something else happens. You have just heard the last item or two and they are fresh in your mind, so you can usually repeat them back almost without thinking. Thus the early items are remembered because your mind is clean, with no other items to interfere, and the last items are remembered because they are still fresh in your memory.

Eidetic Imagery or Photographic Memory

A favorite character in spy movies is someone who can look at a page for an instant and remember it perfectly months later. Such people are said to have "photographic memory." In fact, some people do have the ability to form visual images and recall those images so that they can, in a sense, look at the original page as if it were in front of them. This is called eidetic imagery, or more popularly photographic memory.

Though rare, eidetic imagery is much more common among children than adults; in fact, quite a few young children do have this ability. Almost all of them lose it as they get older, however, so if you want a really good spy with perfect memory, you will probably have to find a child.

Eidetic imagery is truly remarkable. Shown a picture with hundreds of objects, people with eidetic imagery can list every item in the picture even an hour after the picture has been removed from view. They can actually count the number of columns on a building in the picture and recite a passage perfectly. But, after all is said and done, eidetic imagery is mainly a cute trick. For some reason, such memories are not as useful as one might imagine. People are unable to use them the way they might use regular memories—it is as if they have a picture in front of them but can only look at the picture, not employ the information from it. Thus eidetic imagery is terrific for memorizing lists of terms or dates (making it great for school tasks and therefore for young children) but not so helpful for actual thinking (and so presumably less useful for adults). Still, it sure would be nice to have it.

Memory Plays Tricks

Suppose you hear about a robbery in which two people go into a bank, walk up to the teller's window, hand the teller a note, stuff money into leather suitcases they are carrying, and walk slowly out of the bank. A few days later you are asked by the police exactly what you heard about the robbery. Now don't look back! Do you remember if they walked into the bank? Do you remember if they handed the teller a note? Did the teller give them any money? How much? Did they run or walk out of the bank? Now, you probably remembered everything correctly, but maybe you didn't. For example, if you said the teller gave them money, you were wrong. There was nothing in the story about the teller handing over money. As a matter of fact, the teller probably did give them money, because otherwise, how did they get it? But you were asked only to remember exactly what you heard—not to make assumptions, no matter how logical. Many people under these circumstances do draw conclusions rather than just remember, especially if they actually saw a crime, were excited, and are then under pressure in a courtroom.

Psychologists call this constructive memory—we reconstruct our experience basing our memories in part on the actual experience, in part on the few items we remember well, and in part on what makes sense. Naturally, the teller probably gave them money, but maybe they reached over and took it. The point is that this may be remembered because it is probably true, not because you actually heard it.

In fact, this constructive memory is quite a problem in dealing with testimony in court, especially eyewitness testimony. There is always the chance that the witness is remembering what ought to have happened—what he or she thinks probably happened, rather than what he or she saw. The witness is not lying, nor deliberately making it up—the witness is honestly remembering it, but the memory is playing tricks. And how the witness was questioned originally about the event may influence the memory. For example, in one study people were shown a film of a traffic accident and then asked how fast the red car was going when the other cars collided. Later they were asked if they saw a red car. Actually there was no red car and they never saw one. But those who had been asked originally about the red car swore later that they had seen one. Memory plays tricks and in court you better be sure you know what questions the witnesses were asked immediately after the event, because those tricks of memory can be influenced by the questions.

Idiot Savants—Mathematical Wizards

Can you multiply 534 by 685 in your head? How about 79,532,853 by 93,758,479? Seems impossible, yet there are people who can do this kind of wizardry. And they are not fakes; no one offstage has a calculator and is feeding them the answers. They really do these mathematical calculations in their heads. Moreover, they do them incredibly quickly (the second calculation above was done accurately in less than a minute; one wizard found the cube root of a nine-digit number almost instantly). We do not understand exactly how they manage this, but we do know some curious facts about these wizards.

First, some of them are not especially smart in any other way. In fact, some are mentally retarded except for this exceptional ability. These so-called idiot savants may not even be able to read, or understand simple ideas, but they sure can calculate. Some of them also have other strange skills—such as knowing what day of the week a particular date fell on in any year in centuries.

Second, the math does involve what might be called tricks. The best of the wizards know some simple rules of multiplication and division, they have memorized the multiplication table up to 999 times 999, they understand about square and cube roots better than most of us do, and they have a fascination for numbers that helps them realize all sorts of properties that we don't. Of course, knowing the multiplication table up to 999 times 999 may be called a trick and would certainly come in handy, but even learning it is quite a feat. And it seems clear that although these tricks help, they don't really explain how these people manage to do what they do. At least in this one respect, it seems as if their minds work differently from those of most people.

Three Memory Tricks

Suppose you've got to memorize the names of a group of people, or a list of the kings of England for an exam. Memory experts suggest three tactics that will help: chunking, overlearning, and mnemonic codes.

Chunking is taking a lengthy string of information and dividing it into single chunks that have some meaning or make some sense. It is usually very hard to remember a long number such as 719422181671. Dividing this into three groups, such as 7194-2218-1671, doesn't help much because there are still twelve individual numbers to remember. But if you reorganize them into 1776-1492-1812, all of a sudden it is a cinch to remember them, because each of the three sets of four is a familiar date in American history. Instead of remembering twelve digits, you are remembering three dates. Another example of chunking is to convert your telephone number into some meaningful word. For many years, the number to dial for the weather in many places was 767-2676. This is not a particularly difficult number to remember, but it is a lot easier if you convert it to the single word POPCORN (the letters corresponding to the numbers on the dial).

Overlearning means just that: practice and practice again. When you can recall something without errors, that's learning. When you keep on rehearsing it after that, that's overlearning. And the more you overlearn, the easier you will remember.

Mnemonic codes are ways to peg information to something that is easy to remember, such as a rhyme or nonsense verse. A well known mnemonic is "Thirty days hath September. . . ." Mathematicians remember the value of pi (3.14159265358) with the ditty, "How I wish I could recollect of circle round/ The exact relation Archimedes unwound." The number of letters in each word corresponds to the number in the sequence for pi. Acronyms are handy mnemonics. The visible spectrum—red, orange, yellow, green, blue, indigo, and violet— suggests the acronym Roy G. Biv.

One drawback of mnemonics is that you may remember the code word and forget what it stands for (Now what did Roy G. Biv mean?) To make them work better it helps to weave hints—for example, concocting a story full of tips. A medical student who had to memorize the cranial nerves might come up with a story like: "At the oil factory (olfactory nerve) the optician (optic) looked for the occupant (occulomotor) of the truck (trochlear). . . ."

I Didn't Say That—Did I?

Ever been to a party where you had a lot to drink, and then the next day you're shocked to hear what you said or did while you were drunk? The same dimming of memory can happen if you smoke marijuana. Both these highs—liquor and pot—seem to create partial amnesias by interfering with one kind of memory but not another.

There are two main kinds of memory: short-term and long-term. Short-term memories are just that—anything we are aware of momentarily. But if we don't rehearse or pay special attention to what we notice, it fails to register in long-term memory. Short-term memory, for example, is where a phone number you've just looked up lodges while you dial the number. If you repeat it over and over, it will pass to long-term memory. Then there is a chance you'll be able to recall it days later without having to look it up again.

When you're high on booze or pot, your short-term memory doesn't work as well. The result is that less of what happens to you registers in long-term memory. So the next day there may be gaps in what you recall doing, saying, and seeing. Oddly, these highs don't particularly interfere with using your long-term memory. So if you're high you can still call to mind details from the past—providing you weren't high when you learned them.

Amnesia

Everyone has heard about people who suddenly forget everything about themselves, who wake up one morning not knowing who they are, what they do, or where they came from. Although this sounds fantastic, some people do suffer from this condition, called amnesia. We do not know in full why amnesia occurs, but we have some hints.

First, there is evidence that a severe shock, especially to the head, can make people lose their memory. In certain kinds of treatment for depression, an electric current is passed through people's heads. This shock typically makes these people lose all recent memories. They may remember something that happened years ago, but will not remember what happened that morning. It is a special kind of limited amnesia, but it is just as real as the amnesia we usually hear about. It seems as if there is a system for preserving memories in the brain, and that a shock of any kind can disrupt that system so that new memories that are not fully learned yet are lost, whereas older memories, which are more stable, are retained.

Second, amnesia can be produced by hypnosis. The hypnotist can tell the person to forget everything that happened during a particular period, and the hypnotized person will in fact forget. Later, on command, the person may remember if asked to. Thus the memories are not gone, but merely lost temporarily. There is, however, no evidence that hypnosis can help people remember things they have forgotten for other reasons. Hypnotists probably cannot help you remember your first telephone number or what day of the week your second birthday fell on—assuming you have forgotten.

Amnesia not caused by electric shock or hypnosis is a very serious condition, but it is fortunately quite rare. When it does occur, most of the time the person will recover memories after a while. And even with complete amnesia, people do remember many practical things such as how to tie their shoeslaces, their language, and so on. Thus they may lose lots of information about themselves, but they do not usually lose the basic information necessary to get along in life.

Finally, keep in mind that amnesia in its true sense happens very rarely. It would be a convenient excuse for practically anything, but it pays to be very skeptical of anyone who claims amnesia—it is easy to fake, but does not occur very often.

Consciousness and Altered States

Most of the time we are in a normal, conscious, waking state (even if we do not always act this way). But we spend much of our lives in different states of consciousness. We sleep for about a third of our lives, we dream while we are asleep, and the processes of sleeping and dreaming are very different from those of wakefulness. Also, there are other states, including hypnosis, meditation, and drug-induced states such as alcoholic delirium or just a mild high. Understanding these other states is important, not only because they do play a role in our lives but also because by contrast they help us know more about our normal state.

"What Three Things Does Drink Especially Provoke?" —Macbeth, Act II Scene iii

"Nose-painting, sleep, and urine. Lechery, sir, it provokes and unprovokes. It provokes the desire, but takes away the performance."

Shakespeare was right about urine: alcohol inhibits the secretion of a hormone that controls urination, making you more in need of relieving yourself when you drink. The more you pee, the more dehydrated you become. Further, alcohol stimulates cells to secrete the fluid inside them, resulting in a dehydrated body and the thirst many people notice after drinking bouts—and during the following hangover.

As for nose-painting and sleep, Shakespeare was right again. Alcohol is a central nervous system depressant: it dampens down the brain's alertness, loosening some controls on how we behave. Alcohol seems to act most directly on the brainstem's reticular activating system, a series of circuits that regulates the level of arousal throughout the intellectual centers in the higher brain, mostly by suppressing their activity. As the brainstem controls let go, the cortex is released from restraints. One result is the feeling of being uninhibited: merrymaking comes more easily, as does lechery. Unfortunately, because alcohol also lowers the ability to respond effectively in other parts of the body—especially in men—"it provokes the desire but takes away the performance." And, at some point, sleep comes more easily to the drinker than does merrymaking.

Have Some Madeira, My Dear

You've probably noticed that different sorts of drinks have different effects: beer doesn't do as much damage (or good, depending on how you view it) as a martini; champagne makes you more tipsy than wine. Partly this is due to how the alcohol is absorbed.

When you drink, alcohol is absorbed into your body and brain from the stomach and small intestine. Alcohol in the stomach is absorbed more slowly and less completely than alcohol in the small intestine below it. That's why you stay more sober when you drink with a meal than when you drink without eating: the food in your stomach clogs things up, keeping the alcohol there longer. The key to the speed of feeling drunk, then, is in what you eat or drink with the alcohol.

A drink high in proof, with nothing else eaten along with it, has the fast absorption rate. Plain water lowers the concentration of alcohol in the stomach and intestine; because water is absorbed along with the alcohol, the rate of alcohol absorption is slower. Food slows the rate of absorption in the same way; milk slows it more than most other foods. Carbonated water, on the other hand, stimulates digestion, and so speeds the alcohol through the stomach to the lower intestine, where it is absorbed quickly. That, in short, is why Scotch and soda is a faster route to inebriation than Scotch and water, and why would-be seducers should offer their companions champagne instead of plain wine.

Hangovers and Other Disasters

The curse of drinkers—the hangover headache—is in fact not to be blamed on alcohol, but rather on "congeners," a byproduct of fermentation. If you're particularly susceptible to headachy hangovers, you might lower your risk of them with the following information: vodka has a very low congener level, as does beer. Wine has about four times as many congeners as do beer and vodka. Whiskey is particularly risky, especially the well-aged variety. Aging increases congeners, and so well-aged brandy or Scotch are likely to have the highest levels of any liquor—and to produce the worst headaches.

Apart from hangovers, alcohol poses a special danger to pregnant women. Alcohol is particularly effective in penetrating membranes inside the body. This includes the membranes of the placenta. When a pregnant woman drinks, the fetus gets an alcohol bath, which is particularity damaging to the developing child. If a pregnant mother drinks a lot, her child may be born with "fetal alcohol syndrome," a sad combination of physical defects and brain damage.

How Drunk Is Dead Drunk?

Just how disruptive and drunk a person may seem depends on how much alcohol reaches the blood stream. Since heavier people generally have more body fluids than light people, alcohol entering their blood stream does so in a thinner dilution than with lighter people. Women, who have a higher percentage of body fat (and so less fluid per pound), will have a richer concentration of alcohol in their blood than men of the same weight. The more you drink, and the faster, the higher your blood alcohol level. In short, a small woman who drinks high-proof booze quickly will achieve the state of blotto much more efficiently than a large man who sips his beer slowly. Alcohol leaves the blood through the liver, which can metabolize about one-third of an ounce every hour.

The more alcohol in your blood, the more unruly you're likely to be. Alcohol blood levels are calculated in terms of the percentage that alcohol represents in the volume of your blood. In most states, more than 0.10 percent or 0.15 percent means you're legally intoxicated. A 150-pound man could reach that level in an hour by drinking on an empty stomach five shots of whiskey, or five glasses of wine, or five glasses of beer. If he drinks all of the above, he's really in trouble. A bigger man would require more booze, a lighter woman less.

A handy rule of thumb for calibrating the effects of blood alcohol levels is found in the "tale of the D's":*

---

*From Ray, Oakley, *Drugs, Society, and Human Behavior* ed. 2 (St. Louis: C. V. Mosby, 1978); modified from E. Bogen, *The Human Toxicology of Alcohol.* In H. Emerson, editor, *Alcohol and Man* (New York: The Macmillan Co., 1932).

At less than 0.3%, the individual is dull and dignified.
At 0.05%, he is dashing and debonair.
At 0.1%, he may become dangerous and devilish.
At 0.20%, he is likely to be dizzy and disturbing.
At 0.25%, he may be disgusting and disheveled.
At 0.30%, he is delirious and disoriented and surely drunk.
At 0.35%, he is dead drunk.
At 0.60%, the chances are that he is dead.

The Lowdown on the DTs

Alcoholics, we all know, get delirium tremens, the "DTs." But contrary to common belief, it isn't pickling your brains with lots of booze that leads to visions of pink elephants, but going without a drink after you've been on a binge.

To be a candidate for DTs at all requires a drinking binge that lasts weeks or months. Typically, when a person goes on the wagon after such a binge, he or she is likely to develop nausea the first morning after with mild hallucinations. Later in the day will probably come convulsions similar to those of severe epilepsy. The DTs don't show up for three or four more days. Their hallmarks are nervous hyperactivity, extreme agitation, and scary hallucinations: terrifying monsters, bugs, herds of pink elephants, and the like. The nervousness and agitation seem to be a reaction to these unnerving visions.

Hallucinations during DTs are almost always seen, unlike those of schizophrenia, which are more often heard. The sights are so scary that the DT victim sometimes runs around in a frantic effort to escape them. The dread and terror of DTs are so severe that about 15 percent of victims die, often from overheating, heart failure, or accidents and suicides.

The symptoms of DTs seem to occur in part because alcohol depletes essential elements in the brain's cells, particularly magnesium. Injections of magnesium will head off convulsions and the DTs that would follow. Barbiturates and tranquilizers such as Valium, which seem to act on the same brain cells as does alcohol, also help stop those charging pink elephants.

If You Drink Don't Drive—But What if You Smoke?

Habitual pot smokers often claim that being stoned doesn't hamper their driving skills—a claim also made by some about drinking and driving. There's some evidence that the pot smokers are right, but not the drinkers.

Several tests have been made (using consoles that simulate a driver's eye view of the road) of people's driving abilities while drunk and stoned. In one study, for example, experienced pot smokers had either two joints or enough alcohol (the equivalent of six ounces of 86 proof whiskey) to bring their blood level to 0.1 percent (see "How Drunk Is Dead Drunk" to get an idea of how drunk they were). Although both the booze and the dope produced pronounced highs, booze proved much more dangerous than dope: scores after smoking were about the same as when sober, whereas those after drinking were a disaster.

But marijuana may not have a totally clean bill of health on the highway. It may have been that these subjects were out to prove they could do OK while stoned, and so tried harder, an ability observed in pot smokers in other situations. Other tests have shown that people who are stoned tend to drive more cautiously—in some cases because slow speeds can seem to be supersonic to the stoned. Also, marijuana does slow reaction time and make people inattentive to the speedometer—effects that can have unfortunate consequences.

People tested while drunk, though, are notoriously aggressive and take risks while driving than when they are sober. Most important, alcohol has been shown to hamper quick responses to emergencies, whereas grass does not. So although we can't recommend driving while stoned, it does seem preferable to driving while drunk—if you have to make a choice.

The Long and Short of Sleep

Most of us rest easy with seven or eight hours of sleep each night. But a significant minority of people are used to much less—or much more. Edison and Napoleon both needed little sleep; Einstein reputedly slept a lot.

Researchers have studied long sleepers, who say they sleep more than nine hours each night, and short sleepers, who get away with less than six hours a night. When their sleeping patterns were compared, the main difference was in the amount of time they spent in dream sleep: the long sleepers spent an average of two hours in dream sleep, whereas the short sleepers spent only about an hour. Long sleepers also took longer to fall asleep and were up more often during the night. What's more, they stayed in bed much longer after waking. Indeed, the long sleepers actually slept an average eight hours a night, although they spent at least nine hours in bed!

People in the two groups tended to have very different personalities. Short sleepers were energetic, worked hard, were sure of themselves, and said they were satisfied with their lives. They complained little, had few worries, and seemed to have avoided problems by denial and keeping busy. The long sleepers, on the other hand, often valued sleep as a solace from their troubles. They had more worries and problems, were less decisive, and tended to complain more about everything, including being in the study.

How Long Is a Good Night's Sleep?

In addition to differences among people, the amount of sleep that is needed depends on many factors. The older a person, the less sleep he or she requires. A newborn infant sleeps on the average of eighteen hours a day. The length of a night's sleep drops fairly steadily through childhood. During adolescence it will begin to approximate an average seven or eight hours per night, although sleep patterns do not stabilize until around age twenty. Throughout the rest of one's life, the length of a night's sleep gradually declines, although it is largely stable from the twenties onward.

The need for sleep seems to vary with stress. Under stress— emotional crises, changes such as a new job, an increase in mental activity, or increased physical exertion—people often change their sleep habits, some unable to sleep as much, others needing more. Emotional, but not physical, stress tends to increase the proportion of the night spent in dream sleep. If you miss a night's sleep, you don't have to sleep twice as long to make it up. When people were kept awake for three and four days straight, they slept twelve to fourteen hours their first night of sleep, about an hour longer than usual the second night, and then normally after that.

How much sleep should you be getting? It all seems to depend on what you're used to. Unless you're an insomniac, sleep researchers generally agree that the amount of sleep you naturally get, and feel you need, is just what you require.

Things That Go Bump in the Night

Have you ever talked in your sleep? Sleepwalked? Had a nightmare so real and terrifying that you'd call it a "night terror"? You're not alone.

One researcher found that sleeptalking is so widespread that— at least among college students—he could not find a soul who had not been told at least once that he or she sleeptalks. What people actually say in their sleep can vary from a single word like "OK" to a lengthy oration. Sleeptalk is more often clear than mumbled; sometimes it is whispered, sometimes sung. Many sleeptalkers punctuate what they say with pauses, as though they were in conversation with someone else. And, like most conversations, sleeptalk is more often bland than revealing.

Sleepwalkers are less common, and are more likely to be children than adults. Sleepwalking occurs during the deepest sleep, not during the period dreams occur. It is generally harmless—waking a sleepwalker may be difficult, but will do no harm to them. Sleepwalking may run in families—one subject in a sleep study reported that at a family reunion he awoke in the middle of the night to find himself and several aunts and uncles assembled in his grandfather's dining room.

Night terrors are much scarier than garden-variety nightmares. Typically a person wakes up terrified, often screaming. During night terrors a person's heart rate can triple in as little as fifteen seconds—the greatest known acceleration short of a heart attack. Night terrors are typified by some overwhelming physical sensation, such as the feeling of being crushed, being trapped, or choking. But if you've never had night terrors, don't worry. They're very rare. Pleasant dreams.

What's in a Dream

One researcher estimates that by age seventy a person will have had about 150,000 dreams. Does that mean 150,000 fascinating, surreal adventures? Not at all.

Our memory for dreams seems to be selective; those dreams we repeat we're even choosier about. The dreams we recall and talk about are typically more coherent, sexier, and more interesting than most. When volunteers in sleep studies are awakened randomly and asked to tell what they were dreaming about, the responses are likely to be prosaic. The single largest influence on what's in a dream is the ordinary events of the day before.

Most dreams occur during the period of sleep called REM, for "rapid eye movement," which is one of several indicators a person is dreaming. While the eye moves erratically—as though the person were actively watching a scene—the major muscles of the body are still. Paradoxically, the person's brain waves are fully as active as they are during waking. Dramatic changes also occur in heart rate, blood pressure, and other involuntary systems—including, in men, an erection.

What Do People Dream About?

Studies of the content of 1,650 dreams—1,000 from logs kept by college students and 650 from people awakened to report their dreams in a sleep study—revealed the following:

☐ **Dream settings are commonplace.** Only 4 percent of dreams had exotic settings; barely 1 percent had "fantastic" settings.
☐ **Dreams are not lonely.** In only 5 percent of dreams was the dreamer alone; in about a third of dreams there were several people present besides the dreamer.
☐ **People are familiar.** More than half the people in dreams are known to the dreamer. Famous people are rare. Rarer still are monsters: only one was reported in 1,000 dreams.
☐ **Activity is unstrenuous.** About two-thirds of the activities in dreams are simple pursuits like talking, looking, thinking, or going from one place to another. Most dreams that focus on physical activity are about recreation, not work.
☐ **Dreams are dramatic.** Themes of misfortune are more frequent than those of success (at least among college students): failure is more than twice as common as good fortune. Themes of aggression occur in about half of dreams, friendliness in more than a third.

☐ Dreams are not sexy. In the sleep laboratory only 1 in every 100 dreams were about sex; in the dream logs only 7 in 100 were sexy.

☐ Emotions are bland. Even when there is a dramatic event, like a fight, the dreamer will not feel the strong emotion that would be associated with it if he or she were awake. When emotions are felt, they are more likely to be unpleasant: fear and anxiety were the most common feelings, followed by anger.

Interpreting Dreams

There are different theories about what dreams mean. Freud thought that every dream meant something, that the objects and events in dreams were symbolic, and that dreams were wish fulfillments—something the dreamer wanted to happen. Jung thought that dreams represented basic symbols in our culture and also could foretell the future for that person. And many psychologists think that dreams are merely stray thoughts dealing with events and experiences from daily life, sometimes distorted but without any special meaning.

Imagine this dream. You are climbing slowly up a long ladder, you start to climb faster and faster, the ladder itself seems to be growing longer, but as you climb faster you get closer to the top of the ladder. Finally you reach the top and keep going, flying through the air and then gradually floating quietly down to the ground.

Freud might see this as a very sexy dream. Climbing the ladder represents getting sexually excited, the ladder getting longer is an erection, reaching the top is a sexual climax, flying is the feeling of pleasure, and so on.

Jung, on the other hand, might say that you are concerned about achievement and success. Climbing the ladder involves going up in the world. You will in fact reach the heights, but then you'll decide to retire or relax and settle down to earth. Or Jung might interpret the dream as meaning you are going on a trip, flying somewhere.

And someone who doesn't believe much in symbolism in dreams might say you are worried about fixing your roof. You hate climbing ladders and maybe you had to climb one the day before the dream or will have to the next day. And you hope if you do fall off, you won't get hurt.

Take your pick—we don't know just what dreams mean. Probably dreams vary a lot. Some have great meaning to the dreamer, some are random thoughts with little significance, some are wishes, some are fears. The point is that there is no easy way to tell what a dream means or does not mean—it depends on you, the situation, and many other factors.

Daydreaming

Although daydreaming may seem a pointless pursuit, research shows that most adults indulge in it every day. The most likely times for daydreams are in quiet moments, such as at bedtime or during long drives or rides, or in waiting rooms (also, more than likely, during boring lectures or meetings). The time spent daydreaming each day peaks during adolescence and slowly tapers off during adulthood—but daydreams persist into old age. Daydreams of the old are more likely to look back into the past than toward the more grim possibilities of the future.

When young children were asked to sit quietly as a test for "astronauts of the future" and then interviewed, researchers could spot high- and low-daydream groups. Kids in the high-daydream group were able to stick it out longer, probably because their daydreams kept them from being bored. They also were more creative in telling stories and had a higher need to achieve. Finally, they were more often first-born or only children, had a greater closeness to one parent or the other, and had parents who played fantasy games or told them bedtime stories.

Daydreaming seems to be a helpful talent. For example, when volunteers for an experiment were brought to a medical laboratory, had electrical wires taped to them, and were told they would soon be shocked, they understandably became anxious. When they daydreamed to divert their attention, their anxiety eased. But when they had no chance to daydream, they stayed anxious. The most adept daydreamers were best able to calm themselves through daydreaming.

What Daydreams Are Made Of

Unlike night dreaming, our daydreams are under our control. Therefore, you'd think they would be racier, or at least more interesting. Think again.

When hundreds of people reported their daydreams to researchers, most said they enjoyed daydreams. But though many of them reported an occasional wild fantasy, the actual content of most of their daydreams was fairly close to every day possibility. Women, for example, frequently daydreamed about clothes and fashions, men about sports. Men reported more sexual fantasies, whereas women daydreamed more often about physical attractiveness. The research revealed several distinct patterns of daydreams:

□ General daydreams were filled with fantasy and curiosity about people.
□ Self-recriminating daydreams contained repetitious thoughts of guilt and depression.
□ Objective daydreams were reflections on scientific or philosophic themes, more often about nature than people.
□ Kaleidoscopic daydreams had little story line, were scattered and distracted, and reflected boredom.
□ Autistic daydreams were ruminations on night-time dreams, and had a similar dreamy, poorly controlled quality.

☐ Neurotic daydreams were self-conscious, repetitive, and self-centered.

☐ Enjoyable daydreams displayed an enjoyment of fantasy and pleasure in using them for finding creative solutions to life problems.

Reading Minds and Other Handy Tricks

Do you believe in ESP—mind-reading (telepathy), moving objects by just thinking about them (psychokinesis), finding lost objects, and so on? Many people do. But virtually all psychologists are convinced that there is no such thing as ESP, that no one can really read minds or do any of the other marvelous feats.

There has been a great deal of research on ESP. Occasionally one of the studies seems to suggest that some people do have ESP. But in every case, careful research has shown that it is not true—the original finding was just chance or there was something wrong with the work or it was actually a fake. No one has ever demonstrated ESP consistently under carefully controlled conditions, with no opportunity for tricks.

Various people have tried to claim that they have these special abilities—reading minds or bending keys, for example. But trained magicians (or psychologists) always discover the tricks and reveal the person to be a fraud. You too can learn to bend a key, seemingly effortlessly, barely touching it—a terrific trick to impress friends, but a trick nonetheless.

ESP is a wonderful notion. It would be fascinating if anyone actually possessed it (though why isn't that person filthy rich from winning at cards?), but alas, as of now, there is no evidence that it is anything but a pipedream.

Is There a Hypnotic State?

Is hypnosis a unique state of consciousness? Nobody knows for sure, but the answer seems to be negative. Rather, hypnosis is a state of mind induced by the hypnotist that can vary from deep relaxation to intense exertion. We say this because of the fact that hypnotized people do not display any distinctive brain wave pattern, one of the surest markers of a unique state of consciousness. Their brain waves aren't much different from those of people in an ordinary waking state.

The classic signs of hypnosis include an increase in suggestibility, an enhanced recall of childhood memories, compliance, and a reduced capacity to test reality. Some skeptics, though, charge that people who are not hypnotized can be induced to do anything a hypnotized person will do. Exhortations and assurances can produce feats such as lying stiff with the head on one chair, feet on another, without the need to hypnotize.

But there do seem to be some special twists of mind that set hypnosis apart from normal awareness. In one experiment, hypnotized people were told by the hypnotist that a third person was sitting in a chair beside them. The chair was empty, but the third person actually was standing behind them. When the hypnotized subjects turned around and saw the real third person, they were surprised and confused by seeing two images of the same person. When the same thing was done with people told to fake being hypnotized, they either said they saw no one behind them or claimed they didn't recognize them. In short, nonhypnotized people tried to reconcile the illogical situation. But hypnotized people used "trance logic," which allows logical inconsistency.

How Hypnotizable Are You?

The going estimate is that about nineteen in every twenty people can be hypnotized to some degree, providing they want to be and trust the hypnotist. The surest sign of how easily hypnotized a person might be is how readily that person complies with suggestions.

Being susceptible to hypnosis does not mean that a person acquiesces easily to a strong-willed person. People high in hypnotizability have two outstanding characteristics: they can

become absorbed easily, and they are open to new experiences.

A stage hypnotist knows how to screen an audience quickly for likely subjects. One technique is to tell members of the audience how easily they can relax through suggestion alone. The hypnotist tells them to relax and close their eyes, and then suggests they won't be able to open them. He or she spots people who complied with this simple suggestion, and picks them to come on stage.

Researchers use a more systematic test of suggestibility to evaluate how hypnotizable a person might be. One such test asks a person to do the following to determine their degree of suggestability:

- ☐ feel as though you are falling backwards
- ☐ feel that an arm is too heavy to lift voluntarily
- ☐ be unable to open your interlocked fingers
- ☐ be unable to speak your own name
- ☐ notice an annoying fly that you want to shoo away
- ☐ be unable to close your eyes
- ☐ feel that you should buy all your friends copies of this book

Somnambules—Hypnotic Virtuosos

Screening hundreds of people with a test of "hypnotizability," researchers spotted a handful—fewer than one in twenty—who were at the top of the scale. People in this group were generally female, between twenty-one and forty-seven, and had at least some college education. This small group, called "somnambules," share a set of talents that marks them as hypnotic virtuosos. For example, asked to regress to elelmentary school, they were able to vividly reconstruct the sights, smells, and sounds of that period of their lives. Indeed, they have the apparent ability to recall surprising details of their lives, back to when they were infants. They can also produce on request hypnotic phenomena such as being insensitive to pain, imagining they are deaf, and hallucinating.

Somnambules seem to have developed their abilities early in

life. Since they were very young, they recall having a very rich fantasy life, to the point where fantasy intruded on reality. One recounted how she was rudely awakened from the tall grass of a meadow to find herself in the middle of a busy street. While as children they frequently became totally absorbed in their fantasy world, to the exclusion of reality, all had managed to bring their fantasy life under control.

As adults, though, more than half estimated they spent 90 percent of their time engrossed in fantasy. Their talent for fantasy has had some repercussions in adulthood: more than half have had false pregnancies with physical symptoms, and three-quarters are able to have orgasms solely through sex fantasy.

Surgeon Hold Your Tongue

Are you really "out" when you're under total anesthesia? Not really, in the strict sense of the word. Although the anesthetic certainly does kill pain, it also produces amnesia, so when you awake after an operation, you almost always have no memory of what went on during the operation or what was said in the operating room.

However, in a way, your ability to hear while under anesthesia is unimpaired. Your eardrum and the rest of your auditory system work just fine and, under hypnosis, patients have been able to recall almost verbatim some of what was said in the operating room while they were under deep anesthesia. In one study, in fact, anesthetized patients wore headphones over which they heard tapes suggesting a quick recovery; these patients got out of the hospital a full two days before another group of patients who simply heard music. While patients will most likely never remember fully what they heard under anesthetic unless they are hypnotized (and not always even then), the messages they receive can have profound effects. For that reason, those who have done this research have campaigned to warn operating teams to watch what they say.

Sex

Is there anything more interesting than sex? If so, whoever discovers it should let the rest of us know. Psychologists naturally have studied sex from many points of view. They have considered sexual behavior—who does what, how often, to whom, and why. They have also looked at differences between the sexes—just how men and women are different, and how these differences, if any, affect behavior. And they have studied how sex differences arise—how little boys learn to act like males and girls like females; and also, whether this is a good thing, how it can be altered, and its implications.

This section does not discuss many specific facts about how people engage in sex. This has been covered in countless popular books, including how-to books, exposés, and so on. Instead we have concentrated on those aspects of sexuality that are of special interest to psychologists because they tell us about how these vital aspects of our beings—sex and gender—affect our behavior.

Truths and Myths about Sex Differences

Boys and girls, women and men are different in many ways. But most of these differences are physical. What are the actual Psychological differences between the sexes?

The few real differences are as follows:

☐ Girls are on average better with words than boys. This difference appears very early in life and continues at least through high school.
☐ Boys are better at math and quantitative problems. They are also better at visualizing figures and shapes, and at visual design. These differences do not appear until school age, and particularly toward high school. But they are quite consistent.
☐ In terms of social behavior, the only major difference is that boys and men are more aggressive physically than girls and women. Any schoolteacher can tell you that it is boys who get into fights, not girls; and as we know, most crimes of violence are committed by men (though women do an increasing share).

However, keep in mind that there are much greater similarities, even on these few things than there are differences. That is, many boys are better than many girls; many girls are superior to many boys at math; and many girls are violent whereas many boys are not. The differences are only on average. Boys and girls are much more similar in all of these traits than they are in, say, height.

☐ Women are not more suggestible than men.
☐ Men are not smarter than women.
☐ Women are not more sociable or more friendly than men.
☐ Men are not more independent, creative, or thoughtful than women.
☐ Men do not have better judgment; women are not more changeable.
☐ Men are not more logical than women.

And so on. Most of these supposed differences favor men over women, and many people in our society believe them. But they are not true. We have no evidence that men and women differ on any of these things.

Have You Got the Time?

Studies of the frequency of sexual intercourse in marriage show that for young couples the weekly average is about 3 times, for couples in their thirties the average is from one and a half to twice weekly, and beyond age 50 the rate is less than once weekly. To put it differently, couples in their twenties have intercourse about 150 times per year, those in their forties less than 100 times per year.

To get an idea of the relative importance of sex in the scheme of things, compare these figures to those for other activities. People travel to and from work more than 600 times each year, Americans eat regular meals an average of 1,000 times per year, and suburban housewives run an estimated 2,500 errands in their cars each year.

To look at it still differently, consider the time invested. Sexual intercourse takes the average couple between 10 and 20 minutes. Taking 20 minutes as the average time, and 150 acts as the yearly average, intercourse takes about 50 hours per year. Work takes an average 2,000 hours each year, and for the 3-hour-a-day TV watcher, the tube consumes about 1,000 hours each year.

So sex isn't very important, right? No, obviously wrong. But how do we reconcile the importance of sex with how little time we spend performing the act? Surely one answer is that counting only the time spent actually in sexual intercourse greatly understates the amount of time we devote to sex. In the first place, sex involves a great deal more than just intercourse. There is getting ready for some time in bed (or elsewhere), playing around, foreplay, after-play, and enjoying the time together after its all over. There is the pursuit of sex—finding partners, dating, and courtship. And there is thinking about sex, fantasizing, reliving sex acts, and so on. Moreover, though there isn't much actual sex on television or in magazines, there is an enormous amount that relates to sex—pictures of sexy people, articles about sex, stories of romance and love, and jokes. So in reality we do spend lots of time on activities relating to sex—it is only the sexual acts themselves that take very little time relative to their central importance in our lives.

Altogether Now

We may be sending each other chemical messages that our minds don't notice but our bodies use as cues. Take the strange case of female synchrony in the timing of menstrual periods.

An old wives' tale holds that women who live together menstruate at the same time. A study of women living in a college dormitory found the tale to be true: as the school year progressed, the timing of menstrual cycles of roommates became similar, and in many cases identical to the day. The synchrony seems to be coordinated by chemicals called "pheromones." When women were exposed to pheromones secreted by another woman who was menstruating, they gradually changed the timing of their periods to cue into the other woman's.

In animals certain pheromones are sexual attractants. A male moth can detect the fragrance of a female moth's pheromone a mile away; dogs, cows, and pigs also use the scent of pheromones as a signal for availability. Another chemical scent signal for sex, *copulin*, is also secreted by human females. But don't look for Eau de Pheromone or Copulin No. 5 in the *parfumerie* section very soon. Neither seems to turn on humans at all.

Whatever Turns You On—I

"Eat your olives, dear. They make you passionate," is the caption for an old cartoon. The search for a foolproof aphrodisiac has a long and hallowed history. It continues to this day, with no outstanding success but some intriguing possibilities.

Egyptian medical writings from around 2000 B.C. describe recipes for erotic potions. Since then a wide (and ghastly) variety of substances have been proposed: bat's blood mixed with donkey's milk, dried salamander, the fat from a camel's hump, a corpse's powdered tooth, turtle's eggs, rhino's horn, artichokes, ground crickets, and parsnips. Although not a single one of these has proved to be a true sexual stimulant, a number of modern drugs have had their advocates.

- ☐ "Spanish fly," or cantharides, is made of powdered beetles. It can cause dilation of the blood vessels in the penis, thus producing prolonged erections. Regrettably, it can also result in inflammation and irritation of the urinary tract, and can cause severe systemic infection. Despite myths to the contrary, "Spanish fly" has no effect on women's sexual desires.
- ☐ Alcohol and some sedatives taken in moderate amounts increase sexuality indirectly by relaxing people and decreasing their inhibitions. But if overdone they inhibit sexual desire, and in men can produce temporary impotence.
- ☐ Marijuana, like alcohol, can relax people and ease their inhibitions, thus removing some psychological barriers to having sex. But it does not increase sexual stimulation, and so is not a true aphrodisiac.
- ☐ L-dopa, a drug that mimics the action of a brain chemical, was used for a time to treat Parkinson's disease, a neurological disorder. Some male patients in their sixties and seventies were reported to have undergone a spectacular sexual rejuvenation while taking the drug. The rejuvenation may have been due to the cessation of symptoms like chronic tremors, however, rather than to the drug per se.
- ☐ Amphetamines and cocaine, some report, increase sexual desire when first taken, although their prolonged use diminishes sexual pleasures because of

their side effects (such as nervousness, dry and in-
flamed vagina, and exhaustion).
☐ Amyl nitrate, or "poppers," produces a drop in blood
pressure, a feeling of giddiness, and dilation of blood
vessels. Use in conjunction with intercourse, it is said to
prolong and intensify the feelings of orgasm. Its most
common side effect: a brief, but splitting, headache.
☐ Finally, potassium nitrate, or "saltpeter," has the reputa-
tion of diminishing sexual appetites—or so go the
rumors in boarding schools. Actually saltpeter increases urination, but has no special effect on sexual
desire.

Whatever Turns You On—II

The common belief is that women are more taken by romantic
situations whereas men are more turned on by explicit portrayals
of sex. But it isn't necessarily so.

In one study of this belief, men and women who volunteered for
a study of sexual responsiveness listened to erotic tapes. While
they listened, their sexual arousal was measured—men with a
strain gauge around their penis, women with an instrument
inserted in their vagina to measure changes in blood flow. The set
of tapes varied in their degree of romance and sexual goings on.
The majority of women, like men, were more turned on by sex
than by romance. In fact, the women rated the sexy tapes as even a
greater turn-on than did the men. The most arousing story line for
both sexes depicted a woman initiating lovemaking.

By and large, people are most turned on by depictions of sexual
acts they themselves might engage in. For women who watched
slides of various sexual situations, the most arousing proved to be
cunnilingus, the least arousing a picture of a nude man and of a
clothed woman. For men, intercourse was the biggest turn-on, a
clothed man the least. Both sexes were unresponsive to sadism and
homosexual acts. Naturally, for people with special sexual preferences, things change. As might be expected, homosexual acts
proved most arousing for gays.

What Do Other Folks Do—sexually?

The sexual revolution has arrived, and we are all aware of it. But just what does this mean? What are people doing, how often, with whom, and so on? It is somewhat hard to be certain, because the only way to find out (short of peeking through windows) is to ask, and some people are reluctant to talk about their sex lives. Others, moreover, love to talk about it but may exaggerate, and you can never know for sure who is telling the truth and who is embellishing a little or a lot. So take the following figures with a grain of salt—they may not be perfectly accurate, though they probably do give some sense of what is going on.

Clearly, there has been a major change over the past forty years in sexual behavior and attitudes. When Kinsey first started research on sexuality, he found that only 40 percent of the males and 20 percent of the females had had intercourse before they were twenty, and over half of the women were virgins at marriage. Now 60 percent of the boys and 45 percent of the girls have had intercourse before twenty, and most of these are quite active sexually. Moreover, almost 40 percent of teenagers have had intercourse by the age of fifteen. In addition, 95 percent of married males and 81 percent of married females have had intercourse before marriage. At least in terms of the relationship between marriage and sexual intercourse, the revolution is here—no longer is marriage considered necessary for sex by most people.

Not only sexual intercourse, but other kinds of sexual behavior are more widespread than before. Behaviors that are still considered illegal in some states are taken for granted by a considerable portion of the population. Oral-genital sex has been at least tried by over 70 percent of the people, and anal sex has been tried by a substantial number, though it does not seem to be terribly popular with most of them.

Despite these changes, sex appears to have remained primarily something that is done in twos, not larger groups, and people are less free-swinging than might have been imagined. About 10 percent of the population say they have tried group sex (meaning more than two), though very few do it more than once or twice, and even these figures may be exaggerated. Mate swapping (or, as it is usually called, wife-swapping—an unfair term if there ever was one) is quite rare, though definitely happening. Perhaps 5 percent of the population have tried it.

Finally, attitudes have changed even more than behavior. People may not do very much more than they did many years ago (though they do it earlier), but they are much more accepting of all sorts of sexual practices. For example, twenty years ago, almost 80 percent of one sample thought that premarital sex was wrong in principle, while only 9 percent feel that way now. And only a little more than 20 percent feel that extramarital sex is always wrong in principle. Most people are cautious about it, and think it can be disastrous for a marriage, but they also think it can sometimes help and that it is all right under certain circumstances. Nevertheless, one basic attitude has not changed too much. Most people still think that sex and love should be linked, that casual sex is either wrong or not very pleasurable, and that one should have at least some positive emotional involvement with someone before engaging in sex with that person.

How Liberated Did We Get?

Back in the early 1950s, researcher Alfred Kinsey rocked the notion with his results from studying the sex lives of 10,000 American men and women. Twenty-five years later, the Playboy Foundation commissioned a similar national survey, to see how things had changed. Here are some of the trends they spotted.

Kinsey reported:

☐ Among the married, 85 percent of men and almost half the women had had premarital intercourse.
☐ Half the husbands and one-fourth the wives confessed to extramarital affairs.

□ 60 percent of men and 43 percent of women had engaged in oral-genital sex.
□ 37 percent of men and 28 percent of women had had a homosexual experience.
□ 4 percent of men and 2 percent of women were exclusively homosexual.
□ 8 percent of men and 4 percent of women had had erotic relations with an animal.

Playboy's update a quarter-century later, in the mid-1970s, revealed:

□ The number of married men who had had premarital intercourse was about the same as in Kinsey's day, but the proportion of women had risen from half to over three-quarters.
□ Men's use of prostitutes had dropped by half from the days of Kinsey's report.
□ Rates for marital infidelity among men had dropped about 10 percent (to 41 percent), whereas for women they were about the same (25 percent).
□ Oral-genital sex rose in popularity, to 66 percent for men and 72 percent for women.
□ There was a steep drop in the rate of sex with animals, to just 3 percent for both men and women—presumably because fewer Americans live on farms.

The Vanishing Virgin

From what little data are available, it seems that around World War I about three out of four women were virgins at the time of their marriage. By World War II the figure had dropped to one out of two. By the 1960s, half of women were no longer virgins by age twenty-one, and by the time of marriage, only one in four was a virgin.

In the good old days, it was common for a groom to have had sexual experience though his bride was a virgin. By World War II, one in two college-age men was a virgin, and by the mid-sixties virgin twenty-year-old males numbered just one in every three. The most recent figures show that the rate of nonvirginity in brides is closing in on the rate for grooms, which is close to 95 percent.

The Kinsey study dealt a blow to the myth of the virginal bride by reporting that 40 percent of women interviewed had reached their first orgasm through masturbation, 24 percent during petting, 10 percent in premarital intercourse, 5 percent during a sexy dream, and 3 percent while making love with another woman.

A Penny for Your Thoughts, Dear

A survey of women's experiences during lovemaking found that two-thirds almost always engaged in fantasies; only 7 percent never did. The ten most popular topics for women's extracurricular fantasies were:

1. having an imaginary lover (movie stars like Robert Redford are favorites)
2. being forced to surrender sexually
3. doing something sexy that is wicked or forbidden
4. being in a different setting, such as a beach or motel
5. remembering a past sexual encounter
6. being sexually exciting to many men
7. watching herself or someone else have sex
8. pretending she is irresistibly sexy
9. struggling to resist before being sexually aroused
10. having many men make love to her

"That Time of Month"

Everyone knows that at "that time" of month women are unreliable, overly emotional, and generally unable to deal with important or sensitive matters. Well, this just isn't true, as we should see clearly from the fact that all sorts of women manage to do complex, sensitive jobs, to do them extremely well, *and* to do them at all times of the month. So the business about women being emotional or unreliable while they menstruate is just nonsense.

But it is not nonsense that women are affected by their menstrual cycles, just as anyone would be affected by the powerful hormones that are involved in these cycles. During their cycles, women's levels of estrogen and progesterone, two important hormones, vary greatly. Just before menstruation the level of both decreases sharply. In some women, this drop combined with physical changes in the uterus can produce severe cramps; other women do not suffer at all. Similarly, some women do get more emotional during this time, whereas others seem not to be affected. However, even those who are more emotional than usual show no evidence of being unreliable or necessarily in a bad mood. It appears that the woman's attitude toward her cycles plays some role in her reactions, but there are also probably real physiological differences.

Nursing Can Be Sexy

Breastfeeding has its sexual moments. Among the common features of breastfeeding and sexual intercourse: the uterus contracts, nipples become erect, relaxation follows, there is intimate physical contact, and blood flow is enhanced in the skin. Apart from these physiological features, sexual excitement can trigger milk release in lactating women. And Masters and Johnson report that twenty-four women in the group they studied who had breastfed were sexually stimulated by it—on three occasions, to orgasm. A quarter of the women who revealed this turn-on to breastfeeding, though, said they felt guilty about it.

The Coolidge Effect

Are men innately more prone to have a roving eye than are women? Feminists may bristle at the proposal, but some laboratory evidence suggests the possibility that new partners can renew a male's sexual appetite when his old partner cannot.

The (no doubt apocryphal) story that has lent the Coolidge name to this effect goes as follows. Supposedly, President Coolidge and his wife were touring a farm. Mrs. Coolidge, walking in a group in front of the president's, saw a bull mating with a cow. On being told that the bull had just finished doing the same thing a few minutes before, Mrs. Coolidge was amazed at his endurance. "Tell Mr. Coolidge about that," she said. Later, when the president arrived at the scene, he was told what his wife had said. Coolidge asked if the cow was the same the bull had been with earlier. The answer was no. Coolidge then remarked, "Tell Mrs. Coolidge that."

Familiarity seems to dim the appeal of a sexual partner—at least for rats. Typically, a male rat is sexually unresponsive for a time after intercourse. But if a new female rat comes along, the male rat will engage in intercourse with her even if he's just had intercourse with another female. The reverse pattern does not hold, however; lady rats prefer familiar partners to new ones. Whether the Coolidge effect prevails for humans is an unanswered question, for lack of suitable scientific data.

If You Don't Stop, You'll Go Insane

In the late 1960s a national sample of college students were asked if they masturbated, and if so, about their attitudes toward it. Four of five college men said they did, and one in three college women. Despite our liberated sexual attitudes and the clear knowledge that masturbation is both natural and harmless, close to half of the students thought it a sign of immaturity, four in ten thought it immoral, and two in ten thought it would hurt their physical or mental health.

Mr. and Ms. Portnoy

For men, masturbation is more common early in life, whereas for women the pattern reverses. The famous Kinsey study of people's sex lives, conducted in the late 1940s and early 1950s, found that a man's first experience with masturbation was likely to be during early adolescence; 85 percent of males reported having discovered masturbation by age fifteen. The comparable rate for females was just 20 percent. The rate for women rises steadily after adolescence, however, reaching a peak figure of 60 percent for women in their late forties. One caution about these figures: people are counted as having masturbated even if they did so just once in five years.

When Kinsey asked how *often* people masturbated, the figures were slightly different. At age fifteen, 85 percent of boys did so almost twice each week; 20 percent of girls did so about once every two weeks. When people marry, their rate drops. Nevertheless, close to one-half of married men between twenty and thirty-five masturbated occasionally, as did about one-third of the wives in the same age group. And though more married men than women masturbate, the women who do so do it twice as frequently as the men.

Does Pornography Lead to Sex Crimes?

The sterotype of a sex criminal is something like the dirty old man poring over obscene pictures and then running out in an overcoat to expose himself to the first innocent young thing that passes along. But in fact, research has found that pornography by and large is not a cause of sex crimes. Indeed, it may reduce their incidence.

A study of rapists, child molesters, and other sex deviants found that they had not been led down the primrose path by dirty books at all. Compared to a group chosen from the community at large, the sex criminals had *less* exposure to sexy books and magazines than did the others-especially during their early life. Pornography did not play a major part in the development of their deviant sexual tendencies. In fact, rapists and child molesters reported that there had been little, if any, discussion of sex in their homes when they were growing up. Their own attitudes toward sex were conservative, and they were uptight talking about it at all. Pornography interested them little.

In 1964 Denmark became the first industrialized nation to legalize hard-core pornography. Doomsayers warned Danes to brace for a rash of sex crimes the following year. But when crime statistics were analyzed, the incidence of sex crimes (including exhibitionism, voyeurism, crimes against children, and molesting women) dropped in all categories. Not only were there fewer sex crimes, but there were also fewer repeaters. Pornography, it seems, may be an antidote to sex crimes.

Feelings and Needs

Our thoughts and behavior are greatly affected by what we know, what we have learned, our skills, and our beliefs. But equally important and often more exciting and interesting are our feelings, emotions, and motives. It is these that make us do something—that impel us to act in one way rather than another. Our wants and needs strive to be satisfied; our emotions make us behave irrationally and sometimes rationally, but always with energy and passion; our feelings are what make us humans rather than machines.

It is easier to study how we memorize a list of dates than how and why we get excited or feel sad. Emotions and feelings are hard to measure, hard to control, hard to analyze. In part, that is what makes them so fascinating. Psychologists are just beginning to understand some of the facts about emotions, even though they have been studying them for this whole century. This section contains some of the bits of information we have about feelings, where they come from, how they are expressed, and how they affect us.

When You Overreact

Your best friend makes a mild criticism of something you cooked and you blow up, getting violently angry and feeling deeply hurt. Your poor friend can't understand what is happening, since the same kind of comment usually has little or no effect on you. Or your spouse says something wonderfully kind and loving, and you just shrug it off with almost no response. Why do you sometimes overreact, and at other times underreact? Often it is a combination of physical and psychological factors that determines your emotions.

Emotions depend on some kind of physical arousal accompanied by some social or personal event. Even if your heart is beating fast and your stomach is tense, you won't experience an emotion unless something happens that is emotional (for example, a man pulls a gun on you, or someone says something sexy). By the same token, if an emotional event occurs but you don't have a physical reaction, you still won't feel an emotion in the usual sense. Now consider what happens if you have drunk five cups of coffee or taken some kind of stimulant an hour ago and your friend makes a critical comment about your cooking. Your body is all hopped up, your heart is beating faster than usual, your stomach is tense, and so on. When you hear the negative comment, you get angry. But you get much angrier than usual because you are already aroused. Normally, you get mildly irritated and your body becomes slightly aroused; if your body is already aroused, you overreact.

Similarly, if you are very tired or drugged so that your body can't react, you will underreact to some emotional event. Yes, it is nice that your spouse said all those romantic things, but you don't really have the energy to get excited about it. So you barely respond.

You should always try to figure out why you are reacting the way you are, especially if you seem to be reacting in either extreme. Maybe it is the coffee, or those pills for your cold, or maybe you are already tense from work. If you know why your

body is very excited or very quiet, you may be able to understand your emotional reactions and make them more appropriate for the situation. You can also do this for other people—if they overreact, maybe they're high on something; if they underreact, maybe they're tired or sick.

Faces International

Everyone knows what a smile means. But does everyone, in every country, read the same meaning in a frown or sneer?

To answer that question, researchers took a batch of pictures to thirteen nations throughout the world, including Japan, Argentina, and New Guinea. The pictures showed people with a wide variety of expressions on their faces. People in each country were asked what emotion each person was feeling. Almost everywhere they agreed on faces that displayed six emotions: happiness, fear, surprise, anger, disgust, and sadness. These six emotions seem to represent "pure" types. But the more nuances of feeling and blends of emotion there were in an expression, the more confused people became in trying to pin down its exact meaning. Not all faces are international.

However, the six pure types stood up to a rigorous test as universal faces. In the 1960s researchers heard of a newly discovered Stone Age tribe in a remote corner of New Guinea. The tribe had never seen a Caucasian, or even a picture. The researchers rushed to New Guinea to test the tribespeople before contact with civilization could contaminate them. Sure enough, the New Guineans could match the same six faces to the right emotions as well as any New Yorker or Parisian.

The Face of Emotion

Most of us think we can tell what others are feeling from their faces. A glance tells us if they're sad or happy, angry or nervous, excited or calm, afraid or interested. But the face can be a tricky signal of feelings.

Although we're pretty good at distinguishing contrasting groups of emotions (we rarely confuse euphoria and depression, or fear and amusement), within emotional groups or when it comes to blends of emotions we make all sorts of errors (see "Faces International"). One difficulty is that facial expressions of certain emotions can seem similar, and that the expression one person makes for a given feeling may be quite different from the expression someone else makes. Great happiness and deep sadness look quite different, but surprise looks a lot like happiness, and disgust looks like anger. Fear and terror can look like excitement, surprise can look like happiness, and sexual passion can look like almost anything.

Just to be sure, you might check with your spouse or lover to make sure just what facial expression he or she uses for sexual passion.

The Forty-six Basic Moves Your Face Can Make

Facial expressions are mosaics of movement built from the activity of the face's many muscles. Researchers have analyzed the facial muscles, breaking them down into their basic movements. Most people, with effort, can learn to move each facial muscle independently of any others. Good actors can play their faces like a keyboard, mimicking any emotion.

The basic moves for each of your facial muscles are listed below. Try each movement described, one at a time. How good an actor would you be?

Lower your eyebrow.
Raise your eyelids.
Raise your inner eyebrow.
Raise your outer eyebrow.
Raise your cheeks.
Tighten your lowered
   eyelids.
Move your lips together.
Wrinkle your nose.

Raise your upper lip.
Deepen the furrow on
   your upper lip.
Pull the corners of your lips.
Puff your cheeks.
Make dimples.
Lower the corner of your
   lips.
Drop your lower lip.

Raise your chin.
Pucker your lip.
Stretch your lip.
Make your lips into a
   funnel.
Tighten your lips.
Press your lips together.
Part your lips.
Drop your jaw.

Stretch your mouth.
Suck on your lips.
Dilate your nostrils.
Droop your eyelids.
Make your eyes into slits.
Close your eyes.
Squint.
Blink.
Wink.

Now see if you can do all these things at the same time.

The Asymmetrical Face: A Clue to Deception

People have long noticed that the halves of a person's face are not quite identical. One eye may sag a bit, or the nostril on one side may be slightly larger. These asymmetries become even more pronounced when a person makes facial expressions. Almost invariably, the parts of one side of the face or the other will move differently: one eye may dilate more than the other, one side of the mouth may droop more than the other, one nostril may flare more, and so on.

An astute observer may be able to use these facial asymmetries as clues to whether a person is feigning a feeling or is sincere. According to one theory, when expressions are spontaneous, the muscle movement tends to be about the same on both sides of the face, or there are about the same number of asymmetries on one side as on the other. But when muscle movements are deliberate, as when we pretend to feel an emotion, the muscles on the *left* side of the face move more than those on the right.

This difference between feigned and deliberate feelings seems to be due to how the brain regulates facial muscles. When facial movements are spontaneous and not self-conscious, they take a route that bypasses the brain's cognitive centers. But when we consciously move a part of our face, the signals to move the muscles go through the cortex, the part of the brain that makes our conscious decisions: The part of the cortex involved seems to have stronger ties to the left side of the body than the right—hence the greater movement of facial muscles on the left.

Why You Can't Wiggle Your Ears

Of course, some people *can* wiggle their ears. But most of us can't. The reason is simple genetics: many people are born with various minor muscles of the face or head missing. It's no great loss, because these muscles are so minor—like the one that wiggles ears—that they are irrelevant to our survival. Even if we have the muscles in question, we may be lacking the nerve endings that would allow us to control them voluntarily. Again, no great loss.

Furthermore, if you have the requisite muscles and nerves, if you don't practice, you'll never be able to do it.

Hey, Mister—Say "Cheese"!

Smiles come more easily to women than to men, from birth onward: infant girls as young as two days show more smiles than do baby boys. When researchers stationed themselves at a train station in downtown Chicago and smiled at every tenth person, women were more likely than men to return the smile. Observations of men and women in impersonal situations, like a short-order food counter, showed that women outsmiled men about three to two. A survey of three thousand pictures from fifteen high school and college yearbooks, dating from between 1931 and 1965, found in every case more smiling women than men. When people were asked who smiles more, men or women, young women aged eighteen to twenty-five were the only group that thought men smiled more—but there are probably other reasons for that!

What's more, social smiles appear more readily on the faces of people who are underdogs in a relationship. In an experiment, when boys and girls were rated for "toughness," and then grouped accordingly, the less "tough" boys or girls smiled—and also gazed—more at their tougher counterparts. But even then the toughest girl smiled more than any boy.

What function does a smile have? One theory holds that early in our evolution the smile was a disarmed threat—a simulated snarl with the anger removed—a gesture of peacemaking. Some theorists propose that this explains why women are more ready to smile—to disarm the bigger and stronger males.

Oh, Look—She's Smiling at Me! (Or Is It Just Gas?)

A baby's smile can melt the coldest heart—but how does a baby learn to smile?

Common lore has it that a newborn's smiles are either random or due to gas. Actually, careful observations reveal that a newborn's smiles occur mostly during dreams; they seem related to fluctuations in brain activity rather than to anything else happening in or around the baby.

Although at birth a newborn can use virtually all the facial muscles an adult can, babies have much to learn about the social uses of the face. The first truly social smiles—a smile at a parent or another caregiver—show up at around three or four weeks. But not until the third month or so can babies give full-blown social smiles whenever they want. By three (or even two) months, some babies can give a smile of satisfaction at mastering some arduous task, like reaching for and grabbing a rattle. By around four months, a baby's social smiles are reserved for the people who care for it the most. And at four months babies start laughing.

We don't yet know exactly how babies learn to use facial expressions to show their feelings. Although infants as young as two or three months can mimic an adult's face, imitation does not seem essential for normal development of facial expression. Smiling and laughing, for example, come "built in," and show up on schedule without baby needing to learn them by imitation. In fact, infants born blind will smile and laugh at about the same points in their development as those born with sight. And by their first birthday, all infants seem able to manage their emotions, smiling for social effects—or having a deliberate tantrum.

Ninety-six Ways to Show You're Angry

Our face constantly sends out messages about how we're feeling. When we're feeling great, we make one set of expressions; when we're feeling down, we make another. Our facial muscles spontaneously pattern themselves to reflect our feelings, but most of the time we're not fully aware of which expressions are on our face.

Researchers have catalogued the various configurations of facial muscles that express each basic emotion. There are, for example, at least ninety-six basic variations of facial expressions that signify anger. One of the simplest is a lowered brow with tightened, raised eyelids, plus a tightening of the lips. Expert eyes, though, can detect scores of subtly different expressions that reveal anger. One of the earliest signs of anger's appearance, they say, is a slight tightening at the corners of the mouth; this sign shows up earlier than any of the others—often before the person is consciously aware of becoming angry.

Happiness is a much simpler emotion to detect. The basic ingredient in facial expressions of joy is tensing of the muscles that pull up the corners of the mouth—in other words, a smile. When a person feels even mild pleasure, this muscle starts to tense long before the beginnings of a smile can be seen.

For your information, here are some recipes for the other basic emotions:

Surprise:	Raised eyebrows, wide-open eyes, and a dropped jaw.
Fear:	Raised eyebrows, a lowered brow, wide-open eyes, and a parted mouth.
Sadness:	Tensed brow with depressed corners of the mouth.
Disgust:	Wrinkled nose with a raised chin, or simply a raised upper lip.

The Too-Scrutable Occidental

The basic emotions are universally recognized (see "Faces International"). But people from culture to culture vary in how they display their emotions. Bulgarians let you know they like what you're saying by wagging their head side to side instead of up and down; Tibetans let you know you're welcome by sticking out their tongues. What is appropriate in Bangkok may be awkward in Auckland. Take the case of the Japanese.

When Japanese and American college students sat alone watching a stressful film, they wore roughly the same facial expressions. But when other people were present during the film, the Japanese controlled their facial expressions, replacing grimaces with smiles. Such differences in the control of expressions of feeling may be the source of the Western stereotype of the "inscrutable Oriental" (or, perhaps, an Oriental view of the "too-scrutable Occidental").

A Traveler's Guide to Silent Insults

Gestures are a language all their own. As with spoken language, the meanings of gestures can vary from culture to culture. Some of the differences can lead to mistakes that can be embarrassing or downright dangerous. For example:

- [ ] Tapping your temple. In America, this gesture means "he's got brains." Or "he's crazy." But in Germany and Italy, the same gesture only means "he's stupid"!
- [ ] The thumb inserted below the top finger in a fist Although meaningless in America, this gesture is a sexual insult in many European countries.
- [ ] Thumb and forefinger in a circle. For Americans, it means "A-OK." In southern Europe it means you prefer sodomy as your sexual activity.
- [ ] Finally, the good old American gesture—a fist with the middle finger extended—is meaningless outside the States.

And They Lived Happily Ever After (Mostly)

A national survey on the quality of people's life has traced definite patterns in the life cycle of couples. The general pattern goes: highly satisfied the first two years, a drop sometime between the second and eighth years, and a strong recovery around the ninth and tenth years. A second low point occurs toward the twentieth year and around the twenty-fifth. But don't give up—those couples who celebrate their fiftieth anniversary report a level of satisfaction as high as for the first two years of marriage.

Sometimes You Can Try Too Hard

Have you ever found that when you are really in a hurry or under pressure to do something, instead of doing it faster, you fumble around, make mistakes, and actually take longer than if you weren't in a hurry? If so, you have fallen victim to one of the oldest principles in psychology, which is that for every task there is a perfect level of motivation. Any lower drive to complete the task and you go slower; any higher and you also go slower. Your best performance is at the perfect point.

For example, putting your key in the lock at home is usually pretty easy. It takes a few seconds: you turn the key and you're in your home. But one night, just as you get to the door, the phone starts ringing. All of a sudden you are in a great hurry, you try harder than usual to get the key in, and sure enough, this time instead of going in smoothly in a second or two, it won't go in, it jams, you drop the key, and so on. You needed to get in quickly, so it took you five times as long as usual. On the other hand, some days you are barely awake, you don't especially want to get home, and then you also take longer because you are moving so slowly.

With other tasks, different levels of motivation are best. In running the hundred-yard dash, you want to be extremely motivated, because trying harder probably won't interfere with your performance; in repairing a watch, you want to move very slowly and easily, so you don't want to be too active; and so on. The general principle is that the more complex the task, the lower the ideal level of motivation. For simple physical tasks, very high motivation is best; for very complex tasks, either physical or mental, low levels are best.

This also applies to the effects of anxiety on performance. If you are very nervous, your anxiety will interfere with performance on complex tasks, but may help on simple ones; if you are totally nonanxious to the point of being casual, your motivation may be so low that you don't try hard enough, which will certainly interfere with performance on simple tasks, and may even hurt performance on complex tasks.

Remember the key in the door—don't be so anxious that you can't function, but be motivated enough so you try.

Subjective Science

These are peak years for science: 90 percent of all scientists ever born are alive today, and they produce scientific articles about their work at the rate of one every thirty-five seconds. One current topic for scientific study is how scientists do science. Early findings pose a challenge to the general consensus of how scientists "should" act. Contrary to the ideal image:

☐ **Scientists are not always objective. They often ignore data that do not jibe with their own favorite theory, and work hardest at confirming their own point of view rather than impartially examining all available evidence.**

☐ **Scientists are not necessarily open-minded. Newton, Pasteur, Darwin, and Einstein all suffered from intolerant attacks by their peers, as more recently did proponents of plate tectonics theory in geology. Journal reviewers have been shown to favor articles that support their personal viewpoints and reject those that don't— even when everything else in the article is identical.**

☐ **The best scientists are not always the brightest. Studies show no strong relationship between scientists' IQs and their contributions to their fields.**

☐ **Scientific integrity is not always beyond reproach. Several cases of outright fabrication of data have** come to light; for example, British psychologist Sir Cyril Burt, who did pioneering work on intelligence testing, made up the data in many of his better-known studies. And the director of the National Bureau of Standards has estimated that there is a "high rate" of biased or symply unreliable data reported in scientific journals.

Are You a Perfectionist?

The drive to excel can be self-defeating. People who won't allow themselves to be anything less than Numero Uno are plagued by their unrealistic expectations for themselves. The perfectionist's lot is not an easy one: perfectionists are fearful of rejection if they fail; are irritated at their own or others' failures to meet their unrealistic standards; and are victimized by illogical, distorted patterns of thought—for example, that they must be perfect to be liked. What's worse, perfectionists don't do so well—for example, they're more likely to drop out of professional training (like law schools), more prone to heart disease, and less likely to be star athletes. A test of insurance salesmen showed that the perfectionists among them made $15,000 per year less than the nonperfectionists.

To get an idea of how much of a perfectionist you are, decide whether you agree with these statements:

- ☐ I'd end up second-rate if I didn't set myself the highest standards.
- ☐ When I make mistakes, people think poorly of me.
- ☐ I won't bother doing something at all if I can't do it well.
- ☐ Making an error upsets me.
- ☐ I could be outstanding at anything if I tried hard enough.
- ☐ I feel ashamed when I seem weak or foolish to others.
- ☐ If I make a mistake once, I shouldn't ever repeat it.
- ☐ I'm unsatisfied if I do only an average job.
- ☐ I'm less of a person if I do poorly at an important job.
- ☐ I'll do better in the future if I scold myself for my mistakes.

If you strongly agree with eight or more of these statements, you're probably a perfectionist. If so, relax—let yourself make some mistakes.

Power—Who Needs It?

The need for power is essentially the desire to have an impact on people, whether through aggression, persuasion, "getting a rise" out of them, or displays of status.

Researchers usually detect the need for power by analyzing stories that people make up for themes that reflect this need. But there are more obvious signs. When college students high in the need for power were compared with others with a lower power need, certain patterns were revealed. For example, some of the hallmarks of people in the high-power group were these:

- [ ] They had more prestigious possessions (compared to students with the same income), such as fancy stereos and cameras.
- [ ] They put name plates on their dorm doors.
- [ ] They liked to try to get away with saying something obscene.
- [ ] They claimed to have had early sexual exploits.
- [ ] They handed in term papers in impressive plastic covers, the paper itself carefully typed.

Men with a high power need have been shown to have higher blood pressure levels than others. According to one theory, this is caused by the tension that is created because these men typically inhibit their impulses to act on their aggressive needs—for example, when angry, they fume rather than openly expressing their feelings. And when suppressed hostility becomes a persistent reaction pattern, it leads to chronic high blood pressure.

The Fear of Success

Why people should fear failure is obvious—but why should anyone fear success? Yet some people do.

The first research on the topic seemed to show that women were more likely to fear success than men. One researcher asked college men and women to complete a story. The women's story began "After her first-term finals, Anne finds herself at the top of her medical school class. . . . "The women typically denigrated Anne's success, for example, by saying that she simply had been lucky, or was an acne-faced bookworm. But men, when asked to complete the same story about a medical student named John, were positive about his achievement. One interpretation of these results was that bright women are afraid of success because they fear breaking the social stereotype that women are not supposed to compete with men—or, worse, to win when they do.

Other findings, though, show that men too fear success in some situations. It seems that if a career is socially typed as appropriate for one or the other sex, then members of that sex view success in that career positively. If not, they fear that success. For example, when the same story was completed by men and women about a man in nursing school, the men's answers showed fear of success while the women's did not. Women whose own mothers worked have less fear of success than do women whose mothers were housewives. These women probably grew up with fewer stereotypes about what jobs—if any—are inappropriate for a woman, and so have fewer worries about the whole issue.

Fears of the Newly Thin

When obese people lose lots of weight, they are, of course, pleased. However, it seems they can also suffer anxieties about their newfound thinness. Interviews with men and women who had each divested themselves of more than one hundred pounds revealed problems such as these:

☐ fear that being more sexually appealing would lead them into emotionally costly affairs
☐ new assertiveness that threatened to break up old relationships in which they had been passive
☐ resentful friends who felt more comfortable with their fat former selves
☐ a sense of uneasiness and unfamiliarity with their own bodies

Researchers warn that fears of this sort may have been responsible for people putting on weight in the first place. As they thin down, the fears surface.

Busted

Men's magazines like *Playboy* subscribe to the motto that, when it comes to breasts, big is sexy. Indeed, when men have been tested on this premise, it has held up: they see big-breasted women as provocative, as having liberal attitudes, and as being "on the mnove."

But what about women with smaller breasts? Both men and women, it turns out, share a common impression of women with petite busts. Compared to their big-busted sisters, they are seen as competent, ambitious, smart—and more modest and moral.

Testing and Intelligence

More than any other aspect of psychology, tests affect people's daily lives. Almost everyone has taken psychological tests at one time or another, and these tests often determine whether someone can go to medical school, get a job, get into a school, and other important decisions. Although there is a lot of controversy about testing of this sort, there is no question that tests are very widely used and are relied on by all sorts of agencies, companies, and institutions.

In this section we deal with some of the tests that are available, with what they mean, what they look like, and what kinds of things they measure. We also discuss intelligence in general, including some of the most controversial questions concerning intelligence, such as whether there are racial differences.

The Varieties of Intelligence

There are many kinds of intelligence, and several thousand tests devised to measure them. Only a handful of these varieties— about thirty—are generally accepted as unique and reliable. These can be boiled down to two general capabilities: "fluid" and "crystallized" intelligence.

Fluid intelligence does not depend on your education or background. It applies to a wide range of activity. One kind of fluid intelligence, for example, is inductive reasoning, the ability to find a general rule from one set of events and apply it to another. Another fluid talent applies to spatial relationships, such as being able to find a missing part of a pattern. Still another is associative memory, the use of clues to aid your memory—for example, remembering the way to a restaurant by pegging it to landmarks along the way.

Crystallized intelligence is more specific than the fluid type. It arises when your general fluid abilities mix with your experiences and education. One simple example is your vocabulary and comprehension of language: the more widely you've read, the greater your word power is likely to be. Another example is your facility with simple calculations: the more you've practiced your math skills, the better you'll do.

In terms of fluid intelligence, a smart fisherman may be just as bright as a smart physicist. But the fisherman will have higher crystallized intelligence in those areas that touch on fishing, whereas the physicist will have higher crystallized intelligence in areas related to physics. Given equal fluid intelligence, the question. "Who is smarter, the fisherman or the physicist?" makes no sense until you ask "smarter for what?"

Because fluidity peaks in a person's twenties, these are typically the years of a person's greatest creativity. For example, half the fifty-two greatest discoveries in chemistry were made by people not yet twenty-nine. But a person's greatest intellectual *productivity* typically occurs later, during the thirities and forties, while crystallized faculties are still growing.

Most IQ tests mix fluid and crystallized capacities in varying degrees and so give different answers to the question of whether IQ declines with age (see "Your IQ: How it Grows and Declines"). If the tests tap fluid intelligence they'll show a decline; if crystallized, little or no drop.

Testing, Testing

Virtually all of us have taken psychological tests at one time or another. We are tested at birth, in school, to get into graduate school, to get jobs, and so on. Psychologists have devised tests that are supposed to measure almost every aspect of our beings, from aptitude to intelligence to personality. In case you haven't run across all of them, here is a representative list of things that have been tested:

☐ verbal intelligence (how good you are with words and verbal reasoning)
☐ quantitative intelligence (how good you are with numbers and mathematical reasoning)
☐ creativity (for example, list as many uses as you can for a brick. The more uses and the more interesting they are, the more creative you are)
☐ aptitude for medicine, law, architecture, psychology, you name it
☐ ability to get along with others (personnel officers love this one)
☐ need for achievement (how hard you strive for suc cess)
☐ fear or failure (whether you avoid things because you fear failing)
☐ anxiety (how nervous you get about certain things; how nervous you are in general)
☐ self-control
☐ femininity and masculinity (how well your behavior and thoughts coincide with typical male and female behavior and thoughts)
☐ androgyny (whether you have a mixed-sex pattern, taking on the best qualities of both sexes)
☐ Machiavellianism (see "When is Dishonest Honest?")
☐ all sorts and varieties of craziness

What's in an IQ Score

Your IQ, or intelligence quotient, summarizes in a single number your intellectual standing in comparison to others in your age group. Your IQ is calculated as your mental age divided by your actual age times 100. So, if a child is as smart as an average six-year-old, but is only four, her IQ is 6 ÷ 4 x 100 = 150. One of the most widely used IQ tests, the Wechsler scale, has separate tables for ten different age groups. That means you can't really compare your twelve-year-old's IQ of 124 with your own: each score is based on a different standard.

An IQ test measures your mental agility on a range of different tasks. The Wechsler scale, for example, includes tests of your vocabulary, math ability, and general information, as well as your speed on tasks like assembling the pieces of a puzzle. It then adds your scores on all these different abilities into a single total. Your score is compared to scores that hundreds of others in your age range have gotten on the same test, and then converted into an IQ score that pegs your rank against the others. Your actual test score is not your IQ; the score has to be compared to the other scores to be changed into your IQ.

Within a given age range, an IQ score is classified as follows:

IQ Score	Classification	Percentage with That Score
130 and up	Very superior	2.2
120-129	Superior	6.7
110-119	Bright normal	16.1
90-109	Average	50.0
80-89	Dull normal	16.1
70-79	Borderline	6.7
69 and down	Mentally retarded	2.2

What's the Mental Age of Your Household?

Sometime in the mid-1960's educators started to notice that students' scores on aptitude and intelligence tests were falling. Many psychologists have proposed explanations for the decline, including the pernicious effects of TV on kids, the permissiveness of the sixties, and even the tests themselves. One simple—but speculative—explanation is based on the premise that families have a total mental age that is the average of all member's, and that the total intellectual environment of a child's home is a major influence on his or her level of intelligence.

The way to calculate the mental age for a given household is simple, providing you know the mental age of each member: you simply total the intellectual level of everyone, then divide by the number of people. A bright ten-year-old can have a mental age of fourteen; a dull one might have a mental age of eight. Adults are given an arbitrary score of thirty. Thus a family of two adults and one child, using this method, will come out with a higher overall IQ than would the same parents with four or ten kids; the children's level of intellectual achievement brings down the average.

This method has the virtue of explaining why first-borns and children from smaller families have higher test scores on the average than do later-borns and kids from huge broods. The

theory also explains why SAT and other scores may have fallen during the sixties: the postwar baby boom sent a spurt of kids from larger families through the school system. The more recent trend is toward smaller families. According to the theory, then, as these kids reach school age, test scores should rise once again.

The Fate of First-Borns

The first child in a family is most likely to stand out, excelling in school and career. For example, first-borns are overrepresented among Rhodes Scholars, among university professors, among medical students, and in *Who's Who*. First-borns as a group have higher grade-point averages than later-borns, and are twice as likely to be National Merit Scholarship Finalists. Of the first twenty-three American astronauts who passed the grueling selection tests, twenty-one were first-borns.

One theory of why first-borns do so well was proposed many

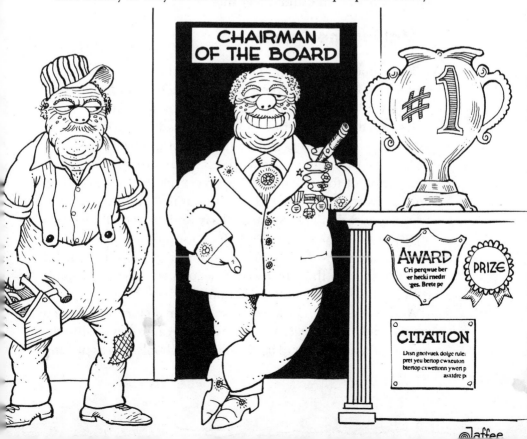

years ago by psychologist Alfred Adler. He theorized that before other siblings come along, first-borns become used to being the center of attention. When a second child is born, the first feels "dethroned." The early experience of a reversal of fortune makes the first-born fear future fallings-from-favor. To avoid them, the child becomes a hard-working striver, a habit that pays off in success.

A more recent theory attributes the first-born's achievements to the fact that the mental age of a first-born's family is higher than it is for later-born siblings (see "What's Your Family's Mental Age?"). The reasoning is that each family's intellectual environment is at a level determined by the average mental age of all its members. A family with two adults and one young child has a higher average mental age than one with two adults and five kids. The richer intellectual tone of a first-born's family, then, gives that child the mental advantage, which is later parlayed into academic and career success.

Making the Grade

Remember that smart kid in your school who got straight A's and always scored the highest on aptitude tests? The kid's probably a great success by now, right? Well, not necessarily.

It seems that school grades and test scores don't predict success later in life all that well. Although many bright people get good grades, test well, and later end up successful, just about the same proportion of those with average grades and test scores end up doing well in their careers. The reason is that aptitude tests and school grades don't assess particularly well the actual skills that a person needs to excel in real life. For example, in a study of outstanding scientific researchers, the average college grade for those in the top third in research success was B–; the average college grade for those in the bottom third was also B–.

Aptitude tests are, however, excellent predictors of how well people will do in college. This seems to be because they test just the sort of skills a person will be graded on in school, such as picking the one correct answer our of four alternatives. Later in life, though, people advance in job status and salary on the basis of far different competencies—exactly which make for the "right stuff" will vary with the particular job in question. A good manager, for example, will need social sensitivity; a good jeweler, manual dexterity; a good actor, emotional flexibility. But in which of these professions does success depend on the ability to pick the correct answer from four alternatives? None of the above.

What Smart Kids Need to Succeed In Life

The 1,528 youngsters singled out in the early 1920's as California's smartest kids have been followed by researchers ever since (see "When Little Geniuses Grow Up"). As a group, these kids grew up to get more education and earn more money and honors than their less bright peers. But not all of them did so well financially or careerwise; a number of them did relatively poorly considering their early intelligence. What made the difference between those who excelled and those who did not?

To answer just this question, researchers compared the one hundred who by 1960 were most successful in terms of income and job status with the one hundred who were least successful. Members of the least successful group were only relatively so: their average income was almost 50 percent above the national average. But the most successful group had an average income almost five times the national average.

Key differences began in childhood: though both groups had about the same IQ, the standouts skipped more grades from grammar school on, were rated as slightly better adjusted by their teachers, and showed greater "will power, perseverance, and desire to excel." These traits became stronger as the kids matured. Adults in the successful group, in recalling their childhood, remembered having parents who encouraged initiative and independence, and they continued to show signs of higher levels of aspiration. In adulthood, the one dimension that mattered most strongly for the successful group was drive and persistence, or for the least successful, the lack thereof.

Creative Does Not Mean Smart or Crazy

The kid who does well in school in not necessarily the one who will paint a great work of art, write a novel, or invent a new kind of semiconductor. One explanation is that the dutiful learning of school lessons may make for high-achieving students but is incompatible with the bent of mind that is likely to spawn a novel creation.

The pursuit of creativity demands some brains, but not all that many. As noted earlier, one study of outstandingly inventive researchers found that the most creative had a college average of only B–. Another study of a range of innovators—architects, writers, engineers, industrial researchers, mathematicians, and physicists—revealed that in only one of these fields— mathematics—did creativity correlate with IQ. Creativity does seem to correlate with intelligence in people with IQs below 120, but above that IQ range, people's creative talents have little to do with IQ scores.

Creative people seem to share certain traits: they are more open to new experiences, less repressed, and less controlled than their uncreative peers. Though during a spurt of creative effort they may become withdrawn and even seem disturbed, they are not pathologically so. Indeed, there is no evidence of a link between madness and inventiveness.

Lie Scales

Some psychological tests ask a series of questions to find out what kind of person you are. They ask about all sorts of things, some personal, some not, and hope that you will tell the truth. But not everyone does tell the truth. People sometimes distort their answers in an effort to look good, or in fact have unrealistic views of themselves. To deal with this, many tests have what are called "lie scales," items that are put in to catch lying.

They work by making a statement that must be false for almost everyone. For example, "I never tell lies," "I am never nervous," or "I have never done anything about which I am ashamed." Now maybe some people can honestly say one or two of these statements is true. But it is difficult to imagine someone answering yes truthfully to many of them. Therefore, by counting how many times someone answered yes, you can get some idea if the person is lying. If so, you can pretty much ignore the rest of the answers.

Race and Intelligence

Some years ago, a psychologist startled the academic world by asserting that there probably were racial differences in intelligence, and that American blacks were genetically less intelligent than American whites. Of course, prejudiced people had made similar assertions for years, but this was one of the first times that a scientist of some standing had made them in a highly publicized article. Naturally, this caused quite a furor and stimulated a great deal of discussion, as well as heated and sometimes violent argument. Now, some years later, the dust has settled to some extent and we can look at the issue with a little less heat.

Although there is still considerable disagreement, most psychologists now feel that there is no reason to believe that racial differences in intelligence exist. That is, there are no genetic factors that cause one ethnic group, one race, or one kind of person to be generally more or less intelligent than any other group of people. American blacks often do less well on IQ tests than American whites, but the explanation for this difference lies not in genetic differences but in economic and social factors. The blacks come from homes with lower incomes, the parents have less education, and naturally the children are less well prepared for tests and for school in general. When black children are raised in middle class homes (black or white), their IQ scores are higher. Also, the tests themselves tend to be written by middle-class whites and thus put blacks at a disadvantage, because some of the questions require knowledge they do not have. This is shown by the fact that tests written by black educators, using material more familiar to black students than to white students gave black students an advantage. Finally, many black students and adults are not highly motivated to do well on these IQ tests and therefore do less well than they might.

Thus the evidence does not support genetic differences in intelligence. Any differences on tests are probably due to social factors. Blacks are as intelligent as whites, as long as social factors and the tests are equated.

Being With People

We are social animals. We spend most of our lives surrounded by other people, and we get most of our satisfactions from interacting with and dealing with others. Social psychology—how people affect and are affected by other people—is accordingly one of the major fields of psychology. It deals with how and why we want to be with others, how groups affect us, why we are altruistic or not, and why we are aggressive at some times and helping at others. It also concerns how we can influence each other—make others share our beliefs, do what we are doing, or vote for our candidate.

We should realize how important other people are to us and how profoundly their existence and their mere presence affect us. If you have any reason to doubt this, just imagine yourself sitting alone in a room and then imagine how your feelings and behavior change when someone, anyone, enters the room. Being alone is different from being in a social situation—with someone else. That is what this section talks about.

Making Friends

What's the most likely reason that we become friends with somebody? You might think it's coincidence of interests, physical attraction, or enjoyment of someone's subtle sense of humor and outgoing personality. However, it's nothing that complex. In this age of great mobility, jet planes, long-distance telephone, and constant travel and moving—in this world where group therapy seems to attract so many of us—the single most important element that influences our choice of friends is simply how close you live or work to the other person.

Although we may remain friends with people even if they move away, forming friendships in the first place seems to depend on closeness. The explanation for this is very simple—you have to know someone in order to become friends, and the more you see the person the more you get to know that person.

Looks and Likes

It should come as no surprise to most people that physical attractiveness plays an important role in liking. People prefer to date, sleep with, have long-term relationships with, and marry attractive people. However, there are some interesting twists to this.

First, as we might have hoped, looks are more important for brief relationships than for longer ones. Physical attractiveness is very important in dating (and probably short-term mating), but considerably less crucial in marriage.

Second, there is a strong double standard at work. Men place much more importance on the physical attractiveness of women than women do on the attractiveness of men. This may be changing in response to the women's movement and changing sexual styles, but as of now, there is still this big difference.

Third, though most people would like to be with the most attractive person possible, there is a kind of matching that goes on in actual relationships. People tend to be with others who are about as attractive as they are. Of course, this is not true for all couples. Often there are large differences. But by and large, the two members of a pair will be considered about equally attractive physically.

Face-ism

The term "face-ism" refers to a bias that seems to pervade our culture: men are judged by their faces, women by their bodies. For example, when men and women are asked to draw a man and a woman, both sexes are more likely to give prominence to the man's face and to the woman's body. This bias seems also to be reflected in the media: an analysis of 1,750 photographs from a diverse range of newspapers and magazines showed that photographs of women devote far more space to a woman's whole body whereas photographs of men devote more space to the face. The bias showed up even in *Ms.*, a publication presumably sensitive to such sex biases.

Familiarity Breeds . . . ?

We like things we know; the more familiar we are with something or someone, the more we like it. This simple relationship seems to apply to practically everything in the world. It is not that we distrust or dislike things we don't know, but that we like the familiar.

Words we hear often sound more positive and pleasant than words we hear little; our language sounds pleasanter than someone else's; familiar faces look pleasanter and we like the people shown more than unfamiliar ones. In one study, people were shown totally unfamiliar words. They were shown some of the words one or two times; others ten times; and still others twenty times. Then they were asked what they thought the meanings of the words were. Sure enough, the more often they had seen the word, the more positive the meaning they gave it. In another study, people saw faces one, ten, or twenty times (only a few seconds each time) and they liked those they saw twenty times

Memo from picture editor:

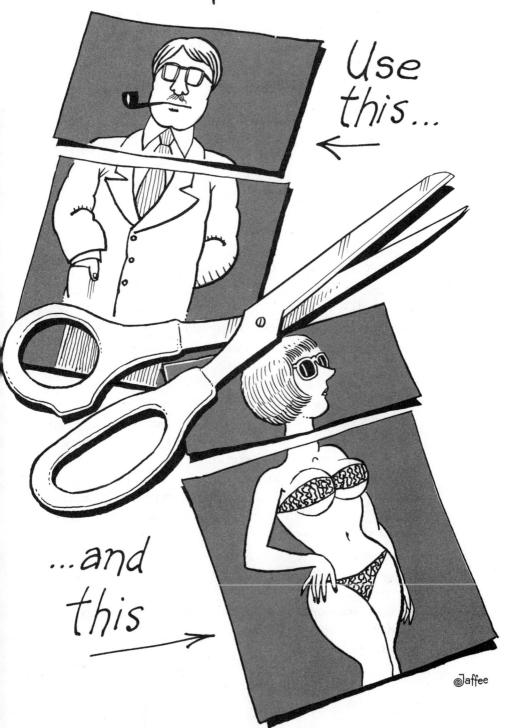

Use this...

...and this

more than the others, even though the faces were all equally likeable. We also like familiar melodies, sounds, art, shapes, colors, and so on more than unfamiliar ones.

"A Fall from Grace"

Your friend George is a charming, generous, witty, sympathetic, handsome, understanding, polite man. So far he sounds wonderful, right? However, he is also known to have murdered someone—now he doesn't sound too good, does he? And even if it weren't murder, but maybe just a little embezzlement or wife beating, you would still write him off. No amount of good works, devotion to the poor, charity, or whatever can balance the single bad act. Of course, if the bad act is mild enough and the good ones good enough, you might still like George, but the point is that the bad act carries so much more weight than the good ones that the latter have to be much greater to outweigh the former. For better or worse, one fall from grace counts more than a dozen halos.

We see this most often in political campaigns, where that one big mistake can cost the election, and no single good action, no matter how wonderful, is enough to ensure the victory.

Consider Edmund Muskie, upset by a vicious attack on his wife, crying in public. Nowadays crying would not be considered so terrible, but even ten years ago people saw it as such a sign of weakness that it probably ended Muskie's campaign. Or Ted Kennedy's brief defense of the Shah of Iran in 1980, which may have lost him a 1980 presidential nomination.

Or Chappaquiddick. . . .

The Halo Effect

Imagine someone described as follows: "warm, intelligent, hard-working, serious, scientific." How positive is your feeling about this person?

Now imagine someone who is described as "cold, intelligent, hard-working, serious, scientific." What kind of picture do you have of this person?

The descriptions are identical except that one person is called "warm" and the other "cold." The evidence shows that this small change shifts the whole impression of the person from positive to negative.

People are either angels or devils—either they have a halo over their head or they have a forked tail. If we know that somebody is very warm and generous, we tend to assume that the person is also intelligent, honest, sympathetic, and hard-working; although these other traits have really nothing to do with being warm and generous, this person has been labeled as one of the angels and has the so-called halo effect. Once someone is given a halo, everything else about that individual is seen in a positive light. Similarly, once you know something bad about someone, that poor individual is relegated to the devil category and every new piece of information is interpreted in a negative way. (see "A Fall From Grace")

This effect is especially important when we are talking about first impressions. On first meeting someone, we are extremely sensitive to certain characteristics such as warmth, and these characteristics influence our whole impression. Moreover, for a considerable time after our first meeting, we interpret new information in the light of the earlier impression. If we had previously decided that a person was an "angel," the halo effect makes us interpret even seemingly negative information in a positive light.

Self-Consciousness

Probably only human beings are capable of being self-conscious, and we seem to have some real problems with it. We ask ourselves how others are seeing us, how we look, whether we are behaving right, whether we are pleasing other people, and if we are doing anything that looks silly. When we are self-conscious, we tend to behave the way we think other people want us to—the way it will make the best impression.

We become especially self-conscious when we are being observed by others—when we are being photographed, or when we are on television. The great skill of television actors is to behave naturally even though millions of people may be watching. Acting natural in front of a camera is one of the hardest things to learn, and most of us never do.

One of the surprising findings of psychology is that having a mirror in a room, even if no one else is present, makes us especially aware of what we look like and how we are behaving, and this causes us to become self-conscious. You think this sounds unlikely? Well, try it for yourself—sit in front of a mirror and try and act natural. Most of us find this very difficult, and instead we pose—even though it is only ourselves we are pleasing in this case.

Being self-conscious has several effects on us. First, of course we tend to look and act awkward, to be stilted and stiff. But self-consciousness also affects our behavior in more profound ways. There is evidence that people who are feeling self-conscious usually act more in line with the values of society or their own personal values than do people who are not self-conscious. Apparently, being self-conscious makes us aware of our values and the values of those around us; we want to "look good" in front of other people (or even ourselves) and so we act more properly. So if you want someone to behave, put that person in front of a camera or even just a mirror—you'll be surprised at the effect.

So Who Needs Enemies?

Watch out for your loved ones: criminologists estimate that two-thirds of all murders are committed by the victim's friends or relatives. The highest risk is from your loving spouse: of these intimate murders, one-half are committed by the victim's husband or wife. Indeed, physical violence is more common between family members than between any other groups of people.

One survey found that close to a third of American couples had assaulted one another within the last year. Wife-beating is very common, but recently, husband-beating seems to be on the rise. Over two million kids had used a gun or knife on a sister or brother, and about the same number of grownups had used similar weapons in fights with their spouses. Close to a million parents had attacked their children with dangerous weapons. Family violence is democratic; it is fairly evenly distributed across ethnic groups, economic strata, and education levels.

The only settings that are more violent than families are wars and riots.

"They Made Me Do It"

If we get involved in a fight, we say it is because the other person was aggressive—we were taunted beyond our capacity to resist— or we give some other external reason. When George gets into a fight, though, we say that he is an aggressive person or has a violent nature. Why don't we attribute our fights to our violent nature? Conversely, why don't we attribute others' behavior to external factors beyond their control?

Whenever we see somebody behaving in a particular way, we look for reasons for that behavior. This process of deciding why a behavior occurs is called attribution—we attribute people's behavior to particular factors or causes. The attributions we make are extremely important because they determine how we see the world, how we interpret what is happening, and than how we respond to it.

The difference between our attributions about other people (George has a violent nature) and our attributions about ourselves (I was forced to fight even though I didn't want to) has a lot to do with our notions of personality. We assume that other people have consistent personality traits—that they act the same way from one time to another—and that these traits determine their behavior. We know that we ourselves, on the other hand, are not particularly consistent. We are often influenced by what is going on outside us, and external pressures sometimes make us act in a manner not consistent with our personality traits.

When Is Dishonest Honest?

Some people are sly, cynical, devious, and wonderfully successful at bargaining and playing games. These people are called Machiavellians after Machiavelli, who in *The Prince* describes how a political leader should act so as to maximize power and influence. Research has revealed the following characteristics common to Machiavellians:

☐ You will probably lose bargains with Machiavellians because they won't follow the rules, whereas you might. They will deal with you without regard to normal morality or ethics and will exploit any weakness that you show.

☐ Machiavellian types will probably also do better than you or I in many social situations for the same reason.

☐ Because successful Machiavellians lack shame about doing things that would embarrass most of us, they can tell obvious lies and then either deny them, or say simply that they made a mistake. Unfortunately, we see this in politicians far too often.

☐ The quality of Machiavellianism is not the same thing as dishonesty. Although Machiavellians find it easier to lie and to take advantage of others, they are not necessarily dishonest in the normal sense of the word—they do not steal or rob banks, or necessarily cheat on exams or even income taxes, any more than normal. An important characteristic is that they are willing to use whatever is possible to benefit themselves, but they still remain within the bounds of the law.

☐ There is no evidence that Machiavellians are bad parents, friends, or anything else—as long as a Machiavellian likes you he or she will treat you just as well as any of your other friends, and maybe even better. As long as someone has nothing to offer a Machiavellian or as long as the person is already giving the Machiavellian everything, the Machiavellian behaves just as well as other people.

The Genetic Argument for the Double Standard

The old-time double standard held that it was "natural" for men to try to have many sexual partners, while women by inclination preferred only one. The double standard has prevailed for many centuries and in many parts of the world—prompting sociobiologists to propose a genetic basis for it.

According to sociobiologists, our genes use us to perpetuate ourselves. The more progeny our genes can induce us to have, the better they fare. Genes are selfish: they'll do their best to get us to act in their best interests.

Sociobiologists argue that polygamy for men and monogamy for women are strategies that represent the best way for members of each sex to ensure the greatest perpetuation of their genes. Among mammals, a female invests more time and energy than a male in the raising of offspring. A woman can bear a child no more than about once each year, whereas there is no limit to the number of children a man might sire with different women. Therefore, a woman will do best to find a single man she can rely on to help her raise her children—and impregnate her again when the time comes. Multiple partners are superfluous for a woman, and, since numerous relationships are likely to weaken the social bonds that make for a helpmate, even undesirable. But for a man, being tied to one woman rather than being free to impregnate many lessens his overall chance of genetic survival. His best bet is promiscuity. We do not suggest, however, that husbands raise this argument for their wives' consideration.

Why Sons Are Genetic Gamble

Sociobiologists put a lot of stock in the selfishness of genes. They use the insatiable urge of genes to replenish and multiply themselves to explain all sorts of obscure facts—such as like why more males tend to be born in times of plenty, whereas female births rise proportionately when times are hard.

Population studies show that to end up with an even number of mature males and females in a given population, we need to start with lots more boys. There are about 130 males conceived for every 100 females, but males die more rapidly than females: by age twenty the male-female ratio is 50-50. Thereafter there are an increasing number of women to men—a set of statistics that seems to have prevailed since Neanderthal times. The male-female ratio seems to vary further with economics. The better off a group, the more males born; the poorer the group, the more females. One major reason is that when a pregnant woman's nutrition is good, she is less likely to abort; thus more males survive to birth with richer and therefore better nourished women.

Now, back to the selfishness of genes to explain fluctuations in the ratio of males to females. In theory, a sexually active male can father hundreds, even thousands, of children, given enough partners and the chance(s). Over her lifetime a healthy female can bear no more than several dozen, if she stays as pregnant as possible. Thus males potentially can pay off better genetically. But keep in mind that daughters and their progeny are more likely to survive hard times; that makes them a better genetic risk when the going gets rough, say during a famine. In such dire periods a male fetus has less chance of surviving to spread his genes. Then a daughter is a safer bet, giving a parent a better chance of at least a few surviving children. And those are exactly the conditions when our genes seem to encourage the birth of women.

First-born and Fears

Are you a first-born? If you are, the chances are pretty good that you have a different reaction to fear than do your siblings.

Experiments have shown that humans are gregarious animals and like to spend time with each other. One of the things that make us especially gregarious is fear. When we are frightened we go out of our way to seek out other people. For example, when there are air raids or earthquakes, we tend to congregate in groups. Obviously, being with other people makes us less afraid, reassures us, and makes us feel stronger because we see strength in numbers. While it is awful to be frightened of something, apparently it is even more awful to be alone and scared.

But those of you who are first-borns seem to seek comfort and companionship when you are afraid even more than do your siblings. Gregariousness also shows up in some other behaviors of first-borns. For example, you are more likely to go into psychotherapy (seeking help from another person) whereas your siblings are more likely to be alcoholics (seeking comfort by themselves with a little help from the bottle). Also, your siblings are more likely to be fighter pilots (a solitary and frightening occupation). Among firefighters, those who were first-borns are more likely to work in a team job such as hoses, while the later-borns are more likely to be laddermen (a solitary job).

Anxiety and Affiliation

Make people afraid and they will seek company; make them anxious and they may avoid it. Although fear makes us congregate, anxiety, nervousness, or concern about being embarrassed does the opposite. When we are anxious about something that is not realistic or about something we consider a weakness in ourselves, we tend to avoid other people.

This tendency was shown in a study in which young men were asked to do something that most of them probably considered foolish, stupid, or embarrassing. These college students, in the full flush of their young manhood, were asked to suck on nipples normally attached to baby bottles. Although this is obviously not a dangerous or frightening thing to do, it is, to say the least, of the ordinary and odd. After they had agreed to this strange act, the students avoided contact with each other and with anyone else. Apparently they were embarrassed by the experience and did not want to show their embarrassment to others.

The same effect may occur when people are nervous about

things such as an exam, a first date, meeting new people, or anything else that makes people anxious even though no danger is involved. Under these circumstances, rather than seeking comfort from others, people hide out by themselves. When the anxiety becomes very high, this isolation can be destructive, because most people can benefit from someone else's help when they are very anxious.

Just an Average Day

A study of minute-by-minute diaries kept by close to 3,000 people turned up the average allotment of time per day by a composite working man as follows:

Activity	Time Spent
Sleeping	7 hours, 43 minutes
Working (on the job)	6 hours, 7 minutes
Watching TV	1 hour, 40 minutes
Eating	1 hour, 29 minutes
Grooming and personal care	59 minutes
Traveling (not to or from work)	44 minutes
Commuting	42 minutes
Visiting friends	32 minutes
Doing household chores	29 minutes
Reading the paper	25 minutes
Hanging out at work	19 minutes
Doing errands	15 minutes
Looking after the kids	12 minutes
Talking to people	12 minutes
Grocery shopping	11 minutes

On the average, working men spend between five and ten minutes moonlighting, cooking, studying, worshiping, listening to radio, reading magazines or books, sitting at bars or cafes, and playing parlor games and sports.

Less than five minutes, on the average, goes to gardening, caring for pets; taking a walk; going to sporting events, movies, nightclubs, or concerts; resting; relaxing; or just thinking.

What Americans Believe

Most of us pride ourselves on being rational, pragmatic types. Yet as a nation we hold to a number of beliefs that have no rational underpinnings. For example:

☐ Two out of three Almericans believe God watches what they say and do, meting out punishments and rewards accordingly.
☐ Close to seven in ten believe that there is life after death.
☐ Half think of Hell as an actual place where sinners endure damnation. But only one in ten sees any likelihood of ending up there.

Marriage and Divorce—The Adults

The divorce rate in the United States has increased dramatically over the past twenty years. Whereas not so long ago almost no one got divorced, now about half of all marriages end in divorce. People may still marry "for life," but they are more disappointed than surprised if their marriage lasts less long than they do. How does this affect them?

In the first place, it should come as no surprise that the period immediately after a divorce is very hard. By far the unhappiest people, by their own reports, are those who are recently divorced. And even after quite a while, divorced people who have not remarried are typically very unhappy.

The good news is that most people do remarry, and that second marriages are as happy as or happier than first marriages. Naturally, you would expect this to be true for the person who divorces and remarries (that is, the second marriage should be happier than the first, because the first was presumably pretty bad). But the encouraging fact is that these second marriages are about as happy as the average first marriage (including marriages that do not end in divorce). In other words, just because a first marriage ends in divorce does not mean that a second one will also be unhappy.

Marriage and Divorce—The Children

A great many divorces involve people with children. It used to be that people stayed together "because of the children." Many still do, even though their marriages are bad; but more and more are getting divorced even though they have children. This raises the very important question of how children are affected by divorce. Although there is not enough research to be certain, we have some tentative answers.

Like their parents, children find the time right after a divorce very difficult. They are torn between the two parents; their lives are disrupted by moving, changing family, financial strains; and so on. In addition, the divorced parents are themselves usually unhappy during this period, which puts additional strain on the children. We should not expect children to take all of this lightly, and they do not.

However, children adapt very quickly. The best research available indicates that by two years after the divorce, the children are doing all right. Compared to a group of children whose parents did not get divorced, the children in divorce are doing just as well. In fact, they are doing better than children who are with parents who are not getting along, which is probably the most important comparison. In other words, if a couple is in a bad marriage and decides to stay together for the children, the children will be worse off two years later than if the parents had been divorced. This is especially true when both of the divorced parents continue to play a role in the children's lives. It seems as if even though divorce is difficult for the children, it is not as bad as parents who fight with each other and do not get along. We should repeat that these are tentative results based on relatively little research, but it is our best estimate as of now.

Positivity Bias

Think of the last movie you saw. Did you like it?

What about the last restaurant you went to. Did you like it?

And how about the last novel you read. Liked it, didn't you?

If someone were to ask you these questions, the odds are you'd answer favorably to each of them. Although we tend to count bad acts more than good ones, there is an odd paradox—for some reason people are prejudiced in favor of most other people. Asked their opinion of almost anyone, most people will say something nice. In fact, asked for their opinion of anything—a person, a movie, an act of Congress, a restaurant—most people will be positive rather than negative. No matter how unpopular a president is, for example, usually more than half the people give him positive marks rather than negative; no matter how awful and unpopular a movie or TV program, more than half the people are on the positive side (not necessarily positive enough to make them watch the show, but still more plus than minus).

One reason for this is that most people are reluctant to *say* anything bad even if they feel it. They are courteous, civil, and pleasant. It is not nice to be nasty. So asked by a pollster how they feel, they say they feel OK about whatever it is unless they truly detest it, in which case they are slightly negative. You notice the same thing when you ask someone how they are feeling. Someone may just have heard that they have to enter the hospital tomorrow, lost their job, separated from their spouse, and played a lousy game of golf, and they still say "OK" or "not bad." And if someone says "terrible," the other person may not even notice. So one reason for the positive bias in all responses is that people avoid seeming nasty.

But there is more to it than that. Even when this is taken into account, most people have positive views of the world and truly do feel that other people, objects, restaurants, TV shows, and so on are more good than bad. Some people may hate a politician of the opposing party, but most people, even those opposed, at most prefer their own candidate. One really bad piece of information about the other person may reverse this, but barring that, people will give positive responses to almost anything.

How to Change Someone's Attitude

Suppose you want to change someone's attitude. One way of doing this is to make as persuasive a speech as possible favoring your side of the issue (politicians do this all the time). The question is how extreme you should make the speech. Should you take a position directly opposed to the other person's views, a moderate position, or one only slightly different from the other person's? Under most circumstances, the moderate position will be most effective.

The reason for this is that the person hearing your speech can do two things—change positions or reject you. To the extent that someone can decide you are biased, misinformed, or just an idiot, there is no reason to take your views seriously, therefore, the person won't change his or her attitude. If you seem reasonable and unbiased, it is much harder to reject your views. And the crucial fact is that people who take extreme positions often seem either biased or stupid. Imagine you think a particular law (or anything else) is terrible. If someone comes along and tells you that really it is a reasonable law and gives you good reasons for believing this, you may not agree immediately, but you may take the reasons seriously, question your own opinion, and eventually be persuaded. If instead this other person tells you that it is the best law in years and there is nothing wrong with it, you may wonder if that person is all there. Anyone who can believe that this law, which you think is terrible, is actually wonderful, must be either prejudiced or dumb. So instead of listening to the person's views and considering them, you merely stop listening and so are not persuaded at all.

Thus, if you want to change someone's opinion, don't disagree too much or you won't have any effect. A moderate position, which disagrees somewhat but not too much, is the most effective.

When Dissonance Can Be Useful

How do you teach kids that it is good to make their beds and brush their teeth, and bad to cross the street against the light? Certainly, rewarding them for doing the right things and punishing them for behaving badly is effective. But how much reward or punishment should you use? The answer is that too much reward or punishment may be a mistake. Giving lots of rewards might seem like a good idea, but actually children who are rewarded a great deal may be less likely to accept your values than children who are rewarded less.

The theory of cognitive dissonance says that we try to behave and think consistently, and that when we don't, we feel uncomfortable. If you want to leave your room a mess but you clean it up anyway, that creates dissonance (because you are behaving inconsistently). But if mommy has given you a great big cookie for making your bed, that is a good reason, so you don't experience dissonance and you don't feel uncomfortable. That's fine so far—Johnny is making his bed and feels just fine about it. However, creating a little dissonance can sometimes be good. If Johnny is making his bed and gets only a tiny reward, he may actually change his opinion about making beds—after all, a tiny reward isn't much of a reason for making his bed, he still thinks making beds is stupid, and so he is behaving inconsistently. He can reduce this feeling of discomfort by deciding that making beds is OK. And once he has done this, he not only will make his bed in the future but will share your values about making beds.

Thus the ideal strategy is to give just enough reward or punishment to get the behavior you want (making beds or not crossing the street), but don't give any additional rewards or punishment. This will make the children (or anyone else) do what you want and also tend to change their opinions to make them more like yours.

Personal Space

Have you ever been in a conversation with someone and felt strangely uncomfortable because something was wrong, but you couldn't pin down what? You then discovered that the other person was standing a little too close to you, and whenever you backed off a little the person moved still closer so that you kept backing up until you were pushed into a corner or against the wall. This is a phenomenon that involves what is called *personal space*. For every kind of interaction between people, there is some perfect distance between them, some amount of space they want around themselves, and violations of that space are usually uncomfortable. In fact, the amount of space people put between themselves and others depends on many things, including where they come from, how well they know the other person, and how they feel about that person.

People from different ethnic groups differ quite a lot in what they consider the normal space for conversation. Americans, Canadians, Swedes, English, and other northern Europeans like lots of space; Italians and Greeks stand closer; and Latin Americans and Arabs stand even closer. Not knowing about these differences can cause serious misunderstandings. Imagine a Swede and an Arab talking. The Swede finds the distance between them too little and backs up. The Arab then thinks they are too far apart and moves closer; and they do a little dance around the room. Meanwhile, the Swede thinks the Arab is being forward, pushy, and too intimate, whereas the Arab thinks the Swede is being cold and impersonal. Yet all the while it is simply a difference in their preferences for personal space.

Men and women also differ in their use of personal space. Women friends stand closer to each other than male friends; but mixed-sex friends stand closest of all.

Perhaps the most important fact about personal space is that it indicates how someone feels about someone else. Standing close often suggests warm feelings, friendship, or sexual attraction. Certainly one of the most common ways of showing romantic interest (before staring into the other's eyes or making more overt moves) is to stand a little closer than usual. The phrase "coming on to someone" (meaning making a sexual advance) may originate in the fact that moving close to someone can indicate sexual interest.

On the other hand, standing very close can also be an aggressive or hostile act. People who are arguing often move closer and closer to each other, standing head to head eventually. So someone who deliberately moves close to you and has no good reason for doing so may be acting unfriendly, and certainly people often interpret it this way. Thus how close someone stands does indicate that person's feelings toward you, but sometimes those feelings are positive and sometimes negative. If you can't figure out which, you may be in trouble.

Groupthink

Why in the world does a group of obviously smart, educated, knowledgeable, and concerned people sometimes make an absolutely idiotic, crazy decision? For example, why did John Kennedy and his advisers go ahead with the Bay of Pigs Invasion in Cuba when, in retrospect, it seems as if anyone could have told them it was bound to be a disaster? According to one theory, the answer may be a phenomenon called "groupthink."

Groupthink is a phenomenon that occurs when members of a group don't listen to anyone outside the group, don't ask anyone else for advice, make a plan while ignoring any information that conflicts with it, and generally do whatever they can to convince themselves that the plan is perfect. While doing all of this, the group members are constantly patting each other on the back, saying how great the plan is, and being very careful never to say anything negative about the plan. It is almost as if they are little kids playing a game and they don't want anything to interfere with it.

While planning the Bay of Pigs, Kennedy's planning group isolated itself from outside influences. It did not even bother to check on the most basic information. One aspect of the plan was a retreat route (just in case the initial attack was not totally successful). This route was into the Colombray Mountains, where supposedly support was available from anti-Castro forces. This sounds fine, but apparently no one even glanced at a map. If they had, or if they had asked anyone who knew anything about Cuban geography, they would have discovered that the mountains were sixty miles from the landing beach through almost impenetrable swamp—no one could possibly have reached the mountains, certainly not with a hostile army shooting at them.

Although groupthink may occur sometimes, we do not yet know when and why. Certainly the Kennedy team often made excellent decisions—in general it is considered quite a successful administration. So even if groupthink may explain terrible group decisions, it does not tell us when to expect them and when not to.

The Risky Shift

Give a committee a decision to make, and it will certainly (or so we suppose) come up with a less risky, less adventuresome choice than an individual—right? Actually, research shows that this is not so. Groups often will make riskier decisions that seem wildly adventuresome.

When people are in a group, a process occurs that has been called the *risky shift*. Although most of the individuals alone would choose a fairly cautious or moderate choice, the group as a whole picks a risky choice. It seems that when people are in a group, their natural tendency to take chances comes out. By themselves they might like to take a chance, but they are afraid to or worried about looking foolish if it turns out badly.

The reason for this seems to be that most of us like taking chances, we value riskiness, and we respect people who aren't afraid to dare. In a group, this cultural value placed on riskiness is emphasized and each person is influenced by it. It is almost as if being in a group brings to people's minds the values of our society, and one of these values is riskiness.

However, this risky shift depends on the choice that is being made. There are some decisions for which we value caution. On these, being in a group actually makes people more cautious. It all depends on what people in general value for that decision. If it is riskiness (as it usually is), we get a risky shift; if it is caution, we get a shift toward caution.

Audiences Matter

When others are around, their presence makes us do better at some things and worse at others. Not only people, but also ants, birds, and cockroaches are affected by an audience. When other people (or ants, and so on) are present, performance on many easy tasks improves. Ants dig more sand; cockroaches learn mazes better; and people are better at lots of simple tasks such as lifting weights, responding to a ringing phone, and answering simple questions. This so-called social facilitation occurs because the presence of other people makes us more alert and more aroused, and we try harder. Surely every athlete knows that running times are better with competition, and that a huge audience makes them even better.

On the other hand, audiences aren't always helpful. If the task at hand is complicated, we generally do worse when other people are around (and so do ants and cockroaches). If we are trying to learn complex equations, do our income tax, prepare a really tough dessert, or do anything that takes lots of concentration and has many parts to it, we are likely to do less well if people are watching. The reason for this is that trying very hard and being highly motivated actually interfere with this kind of work.

So if you want to do really well on tests, study the material by yourself, learn it really well, and then take the test with a group.

Cities Are Unhealthy, Right or Wrong?

It is popular to knock cities. Everyone assumes that whatever else might be nice about cities, they are not healthy places to live. But in terms of physical and mental health, this is absolutely wrong. People in cities live as long, are just as healthy, and are no more crazy than people who live in small towns or the country. The rate of mental illness in New York City is actually slightly lower than in small towns in New York State, and people in our Largest cities actually live longer than those on farms. In fact, a good case could be made that it is farms that are unhealthy— people there die younger than those who live anywhere else.

It seems that even though cities may have some problems, such as smog, that are not good for your health, they have other advantages that are good for you. The services in cities, the level of stimulation, and the facilities are usually much better than in smaller communities. You can walk to shopping; you may be hit by a car but you won't be stung by bees, fall off a ladder, or get bitten by a snake; you have to vacuum but you don't have to mow the lawn or spread fertilizer on the ground. So the good and the bad more or less balance each other, and people in the city don't suffer.

Also, though cities may seem zany and impossible to some people they don't make people crazy—or at least, no more than any other kind of community. True, we tend to see more crazies in big cities, but that is because they are more likely to appear in public and because crazy people may migrate to cities, where they will be more accepted. So you may like cities or hate them, but they are not bad for your health.

The "Pace" of Life

People often say that the pace of life is faster in cities than in smaller communities. By this they usually mean all sorts of things, including social life, activity level, noise, competition, and so on. One study shows that the phrase "pace of life" is a perfect choice, because people in big cities actually walk faster than those in small towns. In many communities, all over the world, people's walking speed on the street was measured. Sure enough, there was an almost perfect relationship between the size of the community and how fast people walked. The bigger the place, the faster people walked.

Crowding—I

Crowding is bad for us. It makes us angry, aggressive, irritated, and maybe even a little crazy. Or at least that is what a lot of people believe. But it isn't true. If we define crowding as the amount of space available for each person, the evidence shows that under most circumstances it does not have any of these bad effects and that sometimes it can even be good.

A lot of work has shown that people can do their jobs just as well in crowded rooms as uncrowded ones. As long as the other people do not directly interfere with what we are doing, they do not have a bad effect on our work. Obviously, if we are trying to practice our golf swing, having ten people in a small room will make it harder to practice—they simply get in the way. But for most jobs— reading, typing, taking exams, painting, and so on—the amount of space we have around us has little effect on how well we do.

Well, sure but what about the more psychological effects? Doesn't crowding make us irritable, doesn't it lead to crime and craziness? The answer seems to be no. People who live or work in crowded environments are no crazier, no more irritable, and in fact no less healthy than those who live elsewhere. Experiments in which people were put in small rooms with other people or larger rooms with the same number of people found that aggression was not related to the size of the room. The amount of space did not affect anger, aggressiveness, or mood. The people were just as happy in the small room as the large one—and the rooms were very crowded, only a few square feet per person. So, in general, crowding does not have either good or bad effects—it can have both, but it depends on the situation.

Crowding—II

It seems as if men and women react differently to crowding. In several studies, groups of men became aggressive and liked each other less when they were crowded, but groups of women actually became less aggressive and liked each other more when they were crowded. Apparently, the men saw the situation as competitive and reacted negatively to crowding, whereas the women saw the situation as friendly and intimate and preferred the crowded rooms.

It has also been suggested that crowding intensifies our reactions, whatever those reactions may be. If we are friendly in a large room, we are friendlier in a small room; if we are angry in a large room, increase the crowding and we become angrier. Whatever we may be feeling when we are not crowded, we feel it more strongly when we are crowded. And so if we are feeling good, crowding may make us feel better; if we are feeling bad, it may make us feel worse.

We can see this happening at parties and other social situations. If we are at a good party, like the other people, and are having a good time, typically it is an even better party if there isn't too much space for the number of people. Thirty people in a huge room have a hard time having a lot of fun—it makes for a dead party. In less space, where thirty people are more crowded, it is a livelier party. But if it is an awful party with awful people, we would just as soon have lots of space because we don't really want to interact with the people anyway. Also, formal, serious parties need lots of space because they are supposed to be quiet and nonintimate; informal, fun-type parties need less space to make them lively and intimate. So plan your parties accordingly—and never have too much space for the number of people.

Crowding and Crime

It has sometimes been suggested that the great increase in crime that has occurred over the past twenty years has been caused by overcrowding. The argument goes that there are more people, they are living in more crowded houses, and they are crowded more into the cities, and that all this crowding makes them commit crimes. This may sound reasonable, but the evidence shows that it is incorrect—crowding does not cause crime, and the increase in crime is certainly not due to an increase in crowding.

Research has been done comparing crowded cities with uncrowded ones, and crowded parts of cities with less densely populated parts. Almost without exception this work finds that the degree of crowding is not related to the amount of crime, once income has been taken into account. That is, poor people tend to live in more crowded areas, and poor people also commit most of the crimes; when income levels are equated, crowding is not related to crime.

One way of looking at this is to consider what has happened to crime rates and population density in our cities over the past twenty years. The amount of crowding has gone down a great deal—there are fewer people in most of our cities, and those that are there live in larger houses or apartments than they used to. So there is less crowding on the streets and in the stores (because there are fewer people per square mile), and less crowding in homes (because the homes are bigger). Yet during this same period, as everyone knows, crime rates have risen incredibly. Obviously, if crowding is decreasing and the crime rate is increasing, it cannot be crowding that is causing the crime.

Apartment Living—Unhealthy for Humans?

Although most of the people in the world live in houses, a great many live in apartments, especially in the United States. And quite a few of these live in high-rise buildings—eight, ten, twenty, or even thirty stories high. Is this a healthy way for a person to live? After all, we are land creatures—we like to have our feet on the ground, and we are used to looking up into trees, not down into them. Besides, isn't it strange and unhealthy to live with so many other people sharing the same building, and to be in the position that you could be trapped in your building if there were a fire or electrical blackout? Aren't these huge buildings impersonal and cold? All of these are sensible, reasonable questions. But by all accounts there is nothing unhealthy or abnormal about living in high-rise buildings. People in them generally are just as satisfied, content, calm, and happy as those who live in low-rise apartments or private homes.

Some high-rise apartments, especially those built for people with little money, have admittedly been disasters, and these have given all high-rises a bad name. These buildings were built poorly, were not maintained, and eventually deteriorated to the point that they were barely inhabitable. In one instance, in fact, the government decided to destroy the building rather than try to renovate it. They dynamited the whole thing and started again from scratch.

But millions of people live contentedly in high-rise buildings, and in many cities the most desirable and sought-after apartments are on the very tops of enormous buildings. People are willing to pay hundreds of dollars extra to be on the thirtieth floor instead of the fifth. So though high-rise buildings may sometimes be bad places to live, there is nothing inherently bad about them.

Noise—How Harmful Is It?

We used to think that loud noise was very bad for people—that it made them irritable and tense, interfered with their work, and was generally unhealthy. Although it is true that many people dislike loud noise, research indicates that it has much smaller effects than we thought and that the effects are quite complicated.

The first thing psychologists found out was that people get used to noise very quickly. Yes, for a brief time, loud noise interferes with work and is irritating. But very quickly—within a few minutes—most people adjust to the noise, stop being irritated by it, and do their work perfectly well even though the noise continues (and this experiment involved very loud noises that were unpleasant sounding, not lovely music or the chirping of crickets).

The second finding was that it was not so much the loudness of the noise that mattered but how predictable it was. When the noise came in steady, regular bursts or simply continued throughout, it had little effect. The only time the noise was somewhat harmful was when it was irregular, occurring in bursts at unpredictable intervals. Then, although people could work just as well while the noise was on, later their performance suffered—probably because it took so much concentration and energy to work during the noise that eventually they got worn out and worked less well. So the lesson here is that the steady sound of typing or even construction will have little bad effect, but the sudden and unpredictable noise of planes overhead or of cars backfiring can interfere with your work.

There is some evidence that long-term exposure to very loud noise can have some harmful effects. In the first place, if the noise is very loud, such as some popular bands produce, it may affect hearing—indeed, many teenagers suffer some hearing loss because of loud music. Also, just living in a very loud environment may have more general bad effects. One study looked at children who lived in an apartment house that was built over a highway. The noise level in the building was very high, and, of course, there was more noise on the lower floors than on the higher ones. It turned out that children who lived on the lower floors had poorer hearing and poorer reading comprehension than those who lived higher up. Although this one study does not prove that loud noise has these bad effects, it suggests that constant exposure to loud noise, even if predictable, may have long-range subtle effects.

The Foot-in-the-Door Effect

You know those advertisements that ask you whether you want to subscribe to a magazine, but even if you don't please just put a mark in the box and send the ad back. Why should they care if you don't subscribe? The idea behind these ads is that once you do anything for these people, even saying no and sending them back their ads, you are more likely to do something for them in the future. This is called the foot-in-the-door effect, because once they have a foot in the door, eventually you may give them the whole house.

One study on this effect asked people at home to post a tiny label saying drive carefully. Almost everyone agreed and took the label. Then, two weeks later, these same agreeable souls, plus some others, were asked to erect a huge, ugly sign in their front lawn—again saying Drive Carefully. Although people who were asked only to put up the big sign almost all declined, more than half of those who had first taken the label agreed. Apparently, once they said yes to a small request, they had difficulty saying no even to a much larger one.

So if you don't want to give to charity, post signs, put your name on petitions, or do anything else of this sort, it is probably best never to say yes even to the smallest, least painful request of this kinds. Having lost your purity "I never do that sort of thing" you may not be able to say no in the future.

Guilt and Altrusim—Strange Bedfellows

Why do people rush into a burning building to save someone, give their fortunes to charity, and commit other generous acts? One reason may be that they are guilty about some awful things they have done. When people break rules or transgress morality in any way, they tend to feel guilty—and there is evidence that people who are guilty are an easy touch. Guilty people are likely to do any favor asked, give to charity, help out, and generally act like good citizens.

In one study, someone was left in a room with a delicate piece of machinery and told not to touch it. It was very tempting, however, and eventually, out of boredom and curiousity, he moved some dials. The machine immediately gave out a puff of smoke and fell apart. Later the same man was asked to do a favor that involved a lot of trouble. He was very likely to agree, much more likely than other people who had not first destroyed the machine. One transgression led to later altruism.

The explanation seems to be that when people feel guilty they want to make up for it. One way of atoning is to do a good deed. So they act altruistically, help someone out, and then feel like good people again. The evil robber baron, who drives helpless people out of their homes and into bankruptcy and gets very rich, later sets up a huge foundation to help people. He feels better, and we benefit.

Good Samaritans: Altruism Had Nothing to Do with It

You're walking through a city street alone at night and see a mugger holding a knife to the throat of a man. What would you do? If you're the type who would attack a mugger at the risk of your own life, the odds are that you're no more altruistic than we cowards are.

The state of California has a "Good Samaritan" statue that offers compensation to people who suffer an injury or loss while going to the aid of someone in distress. Over a ten-year period, about seventy people have been awarded payments under the law. Although some of the incidents involved accidents such as near-drownings, fires, and auto accidents, many of them were crimes of violence in which a bypasser had intervened at a risk to his or her own life. Researchers found and interviewed thirty-two people who had rushed in to help out despite the personal dangers. They were compared with a matching group who had never intervened in such circumstances. What motivates taking such a risk? The Good Samaritans were no more altruistic than the others (few offered sympathy for those they helped), nor were they lovers of risk. The one strong difference between groups was that the Samaritans were more likely to have had some training—such as karate or lifesaving—that might make them better able to handle such an emergency. They also saw themselves as stronger, and were, on average, physically larger. Finally, in almost every instance, the Samaritans saw what was going on as "something that ought not to be happening and about which someone had better do something now!" So they did.

Bystander Please Help

You are walking along the street and you hear someone call for help. What determines whether you offer this help? We know that sometimes people rush right in and assist people in need, and that other times no one helps at all. One important factor is personal preparedness (see "Good Samaritans: Altruism Had Nothing to Do with It"). Another is how many people are around. The evidence shows that, somewhat surprisingly, people are more likely to help when they are alone than when they are with other people.

In one study, people were sitting in a room when they heard a loud noise from the adjoining room and then a woman saying "Help, I fell, I think my leg is broken—Oh, help." In some instances, only one person was sitting in the room; in others there were two people or four people. The person alone was much more likely to help than anyone who was in a group; and the larger the group, the less help was given.

To some extent we seem to decide what to do by seeing what others are doing. If the other people are sitting there and not helping, we decide either that help isn't really needed or that, for some reason, it would be inappropriate or dangerous to help. So when there is a group, everyone looks at everyone else before doing anything, and since they are all sitting around, they all continue to sit around. The person alone must decide by himself what to do, and is therefore more likely to help.

Of course, sometimes a group will help because there is safety in numbers. If someone has fallen into the water and can't swim, a single person would have to jump in alone; five people could form a chain and each protect the other. Or if there is a fight between two people, a group of ten can try to break it up with less risk than if there is only one person. But assuming danger is not involved, more people often means less help—not more.

Who's on TV?

The world television portrays to you is biased. A study of TV during the 1976–1978 seasons showed:

☐ TV men outnumber women three to one, although there are more women than men in the United States.

☐ TV is a world of teens and young adults. Children are underrepresented on TV, whereas there are twice as many TV teenagers as there are in the population. There are about four times as many retirees in the United States as on TV. The greatest proportion of TV people are in their thirities and forties—they represent two-thirds of the people in the video world, just one-third in real life.

☐ There are twice as many lawbreakers on TV as in the general populace. While one-half of 1 percent of Americans commit violent crimes each year, and under 5 percent commit thefts, 10 percent of TV characters are criminals.

☐ TV characters are professionals, managers, or police three times as often as people in real life. Living is easy on TV: between 40 and 50 percent of TV people have no identifiable means of livelihood.

How Violent is TV?

Some highly publicized research on TV violence concludes that heavy TV viewers were led by the high rate of screen mayhem to feelings of fear and mistrust and to a heightened "sense of danger and risk in a mean and selfish world." Just how mean and selfish *is* the world TV portrays?

By sampling hours of TV during the seasons from 1975 to 1978, researchers came up with a TV violence census. It reveals that:

□ There are forty acts of violence of all sorts during each average hour of TV viewing.
□ Verbal aggression is the single most common kind of screen violence. Hostility, insults, and plain rejection of others occur more than twenty times in a typical hour of TV.
□ Physical aggression has an average rate of fourteen acts per hour. The most common types of physical violence are two people fighting; shootings account for 3 percent of outright violence.
□ Deceit, including lying and cheating, happens an average of four times each TV hour.
□ Saturday morning cartoons lead the way with a glut of twenty acts of physical violence each hour.

On the other hand, there are also acts of kindness, self-sacrifice, affection, and empathy. We're happy to report that the rate of all such positive acts is forty-two per hour—slightly more than the rate of violence. On balance, then, the world of TV is slightly more kind than hostile. Very slightly.

TV Violence and Crime

Although there is lots of violence on television, it is very difficult to decide how this affects the actual behavior of viewers. Many people have suggested that all this violence causes crime and aggressiveness, but the evidence does not support this. Rather, it seems as if violence on television has little effect on how people behave; and that whatever effect it may have is different for different people.

There is little question that people who like to watch violent programs are themselves more aggressive than those who prefer sit-coms or other nonviolent programs. Juvenile delinquents like violent TV; noncriminals show less of a preference for violent TV. But this does no prove that TV *causes* crime—instead it shows only that people who are violent also like violent TV, which is hardly surprising.

The few good studies on how TV violence actually affects us are indecisive. Some kids who have a violent nature may get ideas from TV—such as burning someone at the stake or other bizarre notions—but these kids probably would have committed violent acts anyway. And maybe particularly unbalanced people are driven to violence by TV violence, but there is no evidence for this.

At the moment, in fact, psychologists cannot be sure what TV violence does. What is clear is that its effects are quite small. Certainly there is no reason to believe that violence on TV is an important cause of crime or violence in the real world.

How Much Sex Is on TV?

Sampling from fifty hours of programming during the 1977-1978 TV season, researchers counted references to or depictions of sex. The count for an average TV hour: just about one per.

Nightime

With the West closed as a frontier for growth, time—rather than space—has offered Americans new frontiers for expansion. Since gas lamps and light bulbs were invented, more and more activity has gone on at night. A government survey showed that about one in six people works mainly during the night hours; more than half these night workers start their shifts at midnight or later.

Although the night is thought of as a dangerous time to be up and about, it depends on where and when. Acts of violence are concentrated in specific zones of cities—and in specific hours. One study of Boston, for example, found that fights were most common in an area of X-rated movie houses, with peak hours between 11 p.m. and 2:30 a.m.

But night can be a friendlier time than day, perhaps in part because people share the feeling of being in a risky situation. Daytimers and nighttimers were compared on four tests of helpfulness and friendliness: giving directions, cooperating with a survey, returning a lost key, and being sociable in a supermarket. On three of the four tests, nighttimers were far and away more friendly and helpful than people tested during the day. The single exception was mailing back a lost key. The researcher suggests that the low rate of returning lost keys at night reflects the frontier feeling of the night hours: people out at night feel cameraderie with others they meet, who share their risks, but feel a slight indifference or even scorn toward people out only during the day—and the keys, for all they know, were lost by daytimers.

Who's in Charge of a School of Fish?

A school of fish appears to be a well-run, tightly knit group.
Fish in a school line up and match speed with almost military
precision, aligning with their neighbors as closely as they can
without losing speed from each other's turbulence.

But fish schools, which can number from two or three to the
millions, are temporary groupings. The leader of the school is
determined simply by the direction in which the school happens
to be heading. With each change in direction, a new group of
leaders takes over. In one direction the fish at the front of the
school may be leaders. But when the schools change direction, the
fish at the side will take the lead in setting the pace.

Mental Problems

Unfortunately, just as our bodies sometimes betray us and go bad, so do our minds. Of course, everyone at one time or another is upset, overly nervous, or depressed, imagining unlikely events, seeing ghosts in the shadows, and so on. But some people suffer from mental disorders that are more serious than these minor everyday difficulties. One out of ten people suffers from a mental disorder serious enough for hospitalization sometime in their lives; many more have disorders serious enough to interfere with their lives, even though not requiring a hospital for treatment. Some of these disorders can be treated quite successfully; others are much harder to treat.

This section describes some of the disorders and their treatment. Of course, much of this material is from the field of psychiatry as well as psychology and some of it is theoretical rather than being solidly based on research. Mental disorders are the most widespread condition interfering with normal functioning, excluding perhaps dental cavities. It is fitting that psychologists should study them and that we should include them here.

How Much Stress Are You Under?

Change equals stress. That formula distills the essence of a large number of studies done on stress in the last two decades.

Significant changes in a person's life—even changes for the better, such as promotion, marriage, or birth of a child—produce stress. Why should that be so? In large part any major change means that we have to adjust to new routines, new roles, and new pressures. New job responsibilities, a new marital partner, or a newborn infant all make distinct demands on us and require us to cope with new situations and problems.

The more such life changes we have to adjust to at once, the tougher it is to cope with them all. For that reason, life changes can be taken as a rough-and-ready estimate of how much stress there is in our lives. The more total changes, the more stress. If we have numerous major changes all at once, we are more likely to come down with a serious illness in the months that follow.

To see how much stress you're under try the following test of life change. A total score of 300 or more indicates a high degree of stress. Although it doesn't mean you're definitely due for medical trouble, you'd be wise to take care of yourself.

How Many Life-Change Units Do You Have?

Give yourself the life-change units score that corresponds to each of the events listed below that have occurred in your life during the last *two years*.

Events	Life-Change Units	Events	Life-Change Units
Death of spouse	100	Personal injury:	
Divorce	100	serious illness	53
Marital separation	65	Marriage	53
Death of close family		Being fired	50
member	63	Retirement	45
Jail term	63	Marital reconciliation	45

Events	Life-Change Units	Events	Life-Change Units
Change in health of family member	44	Change in living conditions	25
Pregnancy	40	Major change in personal habits	24
Sex difficulties	39	Trouble with boss	23
New family member	39	Change in residence	20
Change in financial status	38	Change in schools	20
Death of close friend	37	Change in work hours or conditions	20
New job	36	Change in recreation	19
Change in number of arguments with spouse	35	Change in church activities	19
Mortgage	31	Change in social activities	18
Mortgage or loan foreclosure	30	Small loan	17
Child leaving home	29	Change in sleep habits	16
Trouble with in-laws	29	Change in eating habits	15
New work responsibilities	29	Change in number of family gatherings	15
Outstanding personal achievement	28	Vacation	13
Start or finish school	26	Minor violations of the law	11
Spouse starts or stops working	26		

My total life-change units ＿＿

Stress It's How You See It

If you've just computed your life-change units score and come up with an alarming total, read on before you run out to get yourself a drink or call your insurance agent.

Consider this: it's not the event itself that makes for stress, it's how you see it. If you construe a major change (like being fired) in a positive light (say, you were in a dead-end job, and now you can draw unemployment while you apply for better ones), then its toll is much less than indicated on the scale. In general, being fired rates a 47; in your case it might be about a 7.

Apart from your appraisal of events, how you cope with them will also lessen (or worsen) their impact. There are some things you can do something about, if only to get more information. Say you get a letter from the auditing branch of the Internal Revenue Service asking you to explain the number of witholdings you've claimed. If you simply panic and start imagining the horrors of a tax audit, you're in trouble. But if you ask a tax accountant what's going on, you might find the form is only a routine procedure— not a sign you're under IRS scrutiny. You can relax.

Sometimes nothing you can do will change the stressful reality. Then the best bet is to calm yourself as best you can. Research shows that outright denial pays off here. Evidence of this comes from research on patients in hospitals. People about to undergo surgery were interviewed and classified as "avoiding" or "vigilant" types. The avoiders typically showed a disinterest in the specifics of their surgery, and had faith that their doctors would do well and that everything would turn out all right. The vigilant types, on the other hand, were alert to everything they could find out about the surgical procedures they were to undergo, were preoccupied by the slightest details, and made efforts to learn all the medical facts—including the risks. A comparison of the groups after surgery showed that the deniers had fewer medical complications and were kept in the hospital for a shorter recovery period. In effect, denial paid off.

Denial seems to work well as a strategy for coping with stress and danger only in certain circumstances. Vigilance, of course, pays off when it can lead to useful action. In general, denial pays when there is nothing one can do to change a situation for the better. For example, there was nothing the preoperative patients could or needed to do that would help with the operation, save be cooperative.

Next time you're on a plane that's ricocheting through heavy turbulence, then, bury yourself in a good novel instead of scanning the wings for cracks.

The Top Ten Hassles and Uppers

While major upsets like a divorce or being fired are highly stressful (see "How Many Life-Change Units Do You Have?"), life's little hassles also take their toll. In fact, if you have lots of everyday hassles—pressing bills, troublesome neighbors, and so on—you are just as apt to have psychological troubles as if you have major life changes. A study of one hundred middle-aged men and women found that a cumulative index of the hassles in their lives correlated more highly with their physical and mental woes than did their scores on the life-stress scale. But the researchers took into account the "uplifts" in their lives, positive events and happy occasions that make people feel good. Hassles, they found, can sometimes be offset by uplifts, buffering stress.

The ten most common hassles:

- [ ] worry about being fat
- [ ] sickness in the family
- [ ] rising prices
- [ ] home repairs
- [ ] too much to do
- [ ] loss of things
- [ ] yard work
- [ ] money worries
- [ ] concern about crime
- [ ] personal appearance

The top ten uplifts:

- [ ] getting along well with spouse or lover
- [ ] good times with friends
- [ ] finishing things
- [ ] feeling well
- [ ] a good night's sleep
- [ ] going out to eat
- [ ] meeting responsiblities
- [ ] getting in touch with someone
- [ ] good times with family
- [ ] having a pleasant home

Narcissism

Remember the story from Greek mythology about a beautiful young man, Narcissus, who fell in love with himself? He loved to sit beside a pool, gazing at his own reflection. The gods were so annoyed at his vanity that they turned him into a flower that grows beside pools. This way he could look at himself all day long and not break the hearts of girls who were in love with him. Well, there are modern-day narcissists who have much in common with the Greek myth.

Today, narcissists are people who are so self-absorbed, so concerned about their own well-being, that they cannot care much for anyone else. They tend to be very charming and smooth, superficially attractive, and even effective. But deep down they are suffering from a terrible emptiness so that nothing has any meaning for them. They are very conceited, think the world owes them everything, and seek beauty, money, fame, and power. But whether or not they get it, they are dissatisfied. They want everyone to love them, and they demand constant proof of this love. Even the mildest criticism can turn them against you forever; if you do not love them totally you are an enemy. But they do not really care for anyone else—all they want is adoration from others, giving little or nothing themselves.

Narcissism is thought to be one of the major problems confronting people in our modern society. It has replaced some of the older familiar mental conditions. Narcissists are like someone who is eternally hungry but does not really like food; no matter how much he or she gets, the hunger remains. It is sad, but it also is tough on those around them.

Some Sad Facts about Depression

Depression is a common disorder: one estimate it that about one in eight Americans is having an episode of severe depression at any given time. Women are more likely than men to suffer from depression, with three depressed women to every two depressed men.

Psychologists distinguish betweeen adaptive depression (say in response to your dog getting run over by a car) and the serious, pathological kind. It's quite normal, even helpful, to undergo a temporary sadness in reaction to a personal loss. This normal depression, which is specific to a situation and passes with time, is so widespread that it is called "the common cold of psychopathology."

Serious depression is a different matter. There seem to be two types, one based in organic causes, the other a reaction to some life event. Whatever the cause, seriously depressed people are a mess. They feel intense dislike for themselves, dejection, and disinterest in sex or other former pleasures. The criticize themselves, have frequent crying spells, can't sleep well, lose their appetites, are easily fatigued, and are often constipated. They expect the worst, see themselves as worthless sinners, and are likely to entertain thoughts of suicide. Typically, they wear a chronic look of sadness and remorse, their posture is stooped, and their speech slow.

Don't try to cheer up depressed people with a joke: another clinical sign is that they don't laugh.

The Causes of Depression

There are several theories about what makes people depressed. ranging from brain chemistry gone awry to learned feelings of helplessness. More than one of these theories may be correct, even though they point to different causes, because various underlying factors might lead to the same constellation of depressed symptoms. Among the leading theories:

☐ **Catecholamines are neurotransmitters (see "The Brain Is a Chemistry Set") This theory holds that our moods fluctuate with changing levels of these brain chemicals. When catecholamine levels are high, it is** thought, we have a feeling of well-being; when they are low, we feel depressed.

☐ The tendency to depression may be inherited. Some studies have shown that depression is more likely among the family members of someone who is depressed. While suggestive, the findings are not so strong that early childhood experiences or other social factors, rather than genes, might not account for them.

☐ Depression may stem from habitual patterns of thinking. This view holds that depressed people, perhaps in early childhood, adopt a negative bias toward themselves that in later life predisposes them to depression. People who have such a "negative cognitive set" already subscribe to the self-deprecating self-image of depressed people; when they encounter stressful life events, these attitudes blossom into full depression.

☐ Depression may be learned helplessness. One key symptom of depression is feelings of helplessness and hopelessness. Laboratory studies where dogs were put in a situation where nothing they did could help them avoid a shock found that when the dogs were later put in a situation where they might avoid the shock, they didn't even try (see "Learned Helplessness"). This same model has been offered as an explanation of depression in humans: life experiences where people learn a sense of helplessness lead them to give up and fall into a cycle of depression when faced with hard times.

Although none of these theories has been proved, they are not necessarily mutually incompatible. It may be that each of them describes accurately some aspect of the causes of depression, or that each applies more to one type of depression than to others.

The Wild, Wild World of Manic-Depressives

The psychiatric syndrome known technically as "manic disorder" is the flip side of depression. The cycle of a manic-depressive alternates between the depths of misery and self-pity and the heights of high-energy optimism. The culprit will probably turn out someday to be a chemical imbalance in the brain. Although manics typically display an ebullient mood, they can switch to anger if crossed. They go on spending sprees, make grand and unrealistic plans, give people advice about anything and everything, and write novels or music with a frenzy but little if any special talent.

The official psychiatric diagnostic manual lists very specific criteria for recognizing a full-fledged manic episode:

1. There are periods of elevated or irritated mood.
2. At least three of the following are present (four if the mood is irritable):
   ☐ heightened activity, whether social, work, sexual, or just general restlessness
   ☐ extreme talkativeness
   ☐ racing thoughts
   ☐ grandiose ideas
   ☐ little need for sleep
   ☐ distractability
   ☐ impulsive acts without regard for consequences, such as sexual indiscretions, foolish investments, giving money away.
3. The episode lasts at least one week.
4. There are none of the signs of schizophrenia (see "How to Tell a Schizophrenic").
5. There is no known organic cause.

Cures for Depression

One of the most hopeful facts about depression is that it passes. Various treatments, though, can speed up recovery from depression, sometimes practically overnight. Not every treatment works for every depression, but these are some of the most common:

☐ Lithium. A mineral salt, lithium halts the intense excite- of manics (see "The Wild, Wild World of Manic-Depressives"),and lifts depression in cases where it follows the manic phase.
☐ Antidepresessants. Drugs that raise the levels of cate-

cholamines in the brain (such as iproniasid and im-
ipramine) can, over several days, lift depression. They
can also be used in a maintenance dose to prevent
recurrence of depression.
☐ Electo convulsive therapy. Sometimes called "electroshock," this treatment entails shooting an electrical
charge between 70 and 130 volts through electrodes
on the patient's temples for a split second. The immediate result is a seizure, followed by a coma lasting
from several minutes to several hours. Electroconvul-
sive therapy is most effective with extreme depression
in reaction to a specific event. Because of its side effects (including memory loss, disorientation, and, if
overused, brain damage), electroshock has a poor
public image.
☐ Sleep deprivation. Oddly enough, a new treatment for
depression is simply keeping the patient awake all
night, or for several nights at a time. No one is sure why,
but the best guess is that sleep loss resets a basic biological clock that underlies depression.
☐ Cognitive therapy. Operating on the premise that depression results from unrealistic, negative attitudes,
cognitive therapists attack depression by helping
patients reevaluate their plight more realistically.

The Ultra-Clean World of the Obsessive-Compulsive

The psychiatric disorder called "obsessive-compulsion" has
two main symptoms; as you would probably guess, they are
obsessions and compulsions.

Compulsions are impulses that people feel can't be resisted. If
they try to resist, the tension mounts until it is too much to bear.
While obsessive-compulsives may acknowledge that their compulsions are bizarre, they often feel that it's futile to fight them.

Obsessions are recurrent, persistent thoughts that seem to
originate from outside one's own mind. Like compulsions, they
seem to the obsessive-compulsive to be unstoppable. The most
common obsessions are thoughts of violence, fear of getting
dirty, and constant doubts.

The obsessive-compulsive's bent of mind produces some bizarre behavior. For one, many obsessive-compulsives are fanatic about cleanliness; some have been known to wash their hands several hundred times a day, change their underwear every few hours, and carry around sanitizing sprays, which they use to douse whatever they might have to touch. Not all compulsions are about cleanliness, though. Some obsessive-compulsives constantly count things, like the number of squares in a linoleum floor, passing cars, or lines on a sidewalk. Others have the compulsion to touch, whether pickets in a fence or people passing by.

Although many of us possess milder versions of obsessions and compulsions, true obsessive-compulsives are rare. But if you're looking for someone to clean your house or keep your books, a toned-down obsessive-compulsive might be just right.

What Are You Afraid Of? Or, An A to Z Guide to Phobias

Phobia, or simple fear of objects or situations, is fairly common. In about one in twenty-five instances, though, the phobia is so severe it is debilitating; among patients with heart problems the count of serious phobias is one in ten. Aversion for pistachio ice cream wouldn't make you qualify as phobic, but if you stayed away from ice cream parlors to avoid it, you'd deserve the title.

It has long been observed that people become phobic about certain things more often than others. For example, insects, heights, bridges, or public speaking cause more phobias than situation comedies, bunnies, or pistachio ice cream. One theory is that we have a built-in preparedness to fear things with some degree of realistic danger—for example, being bitten, falling, or being embarrassed. Thus while a traumatic encounter in our past may lead to a phobia, phobias are far more likely to happen with those things that we are prepared to fear because of their inherent danger.

For your information,

If You Dread	You Have
High places	Acrophobia
Leaving your house	Agoraphobia
Being enclosed	Claustrophobia
Going to the dentist	Dentophobia
Lightning and thunder	Keraunophobia
Being by yourself	Monophobia
Getting dirty or catch-	
ing germs	Mysophobia
Crowds	Ochlophobia
The dead	Thanatophobia
Strangers	Zenophobia
Animals of any sort	Zoophobia

Hiccoughs, Tics, and Spasmodic Curses

A particularly distressing neurological disorder is a distant cousin of the hiccough. Called "Gilles de la Tourette syndrome" (after the French physician who first wrote about it), this disorder causes its victims to emit occasional outbursts of obscenity. The outbursts can vary from once every few days to several times an hour; they often come in the middle of an otherwise normal conversation. Two of the most common obscenities among English-speaking suffers are "fuck" and "shut up"—interjections that can be particularly alarming to the people they happen to be speaking with.

Gilles de la Tourette syndrome is a type of "myoclonus," a medical term for muscle spasm. The myoclonias range from hiccoughs and tics to epilepsy. All of these disorders are caused by cells misfiring usually in the brain's center for muscle movement. Occasional tics and twitches are perfectly normal though chronic tics are usually a sign of too much stress.

A hiccough is a tic inside your body, a spasm in the nerve that regulates your diaphragm. There is no sure cure for the hiccoughs; they clear up by themselves except in a few rare cases. One hiccough sufferer had them continually for eight years, during which his weight dropped from 138 to 74 pounds. Sympathetic people sent him 60,000 suggested cures. The one that seems to have worked was a prayer to the patron saint of lost causes, St. Jude.

Perversions—I
A Quick Tour

The official psychiatrist's diagnostic manual considers the term "perversions" passe. Instead it uses a newly coined term, "paraphilia," which means that a person is attracted to (philia) a deviant object (para). These deviant attractions are considered worthy of psychiatric attention only when a person (1) is incapable of other, normal sexual relations; (2) forces her or his sexual taste on a nonconsenting partner; or (3) is upset by the attraction itself.

The paraphilias include the following:

☐ Fetishism, the erotic preference for an inanimate object, or the need to use the object to become aroused when having sex with a human partner. Almost any object can be the source of a fetish; among the most popular are lingerie, women's shoes and boots, hair, or some object associated with a part of the human body. Virtually all fetishists are men, and often they are unable to get an erection with a partner unless the fetish is part of the act.

☐ Zoophilia, the preference for or exclusive use of animals for erotic arousal, despite the availability of human partners. The most common choices of zoophiliacs are household pets and farm animals. Zoophilia is rare and getting rarer, in part because of the declining number of Americans who live on farms.

☐ Pedophilia, the erotic preference for prepubertal children, or the "Lolita syndrome." The most common preference among pedophiliacs is for eight-to ten-year-old girls.

☐ Dyshomophilia, the preference for homosexual activity if the person is upset by that preference, or uneasiness about homosexuality. Homosexuality itself is not considered a psychiatriac disorder these days, though it once was. Only those homosexuals who are conscience-stricken by their sexual tastes receive this diagnosis.

☐ Exhibitionism, being sexually aroused by exposing one's genitals to any unsuspecting stranger. This paraphilia seems to occur only in men. Many exhibitionists are married but have an unhappy sex life. Their favorite targets for "flashing" are women and children. Exhibitionists don't want to have sex with the objects of their display; the act itself is the source of their sexual gratification.

☐ Voyeurism, peeking at an unsuspecting woman (or man, though usually voyeurs are males) who is naked, undressing, or having intercourse. The voyeur usually masturbates while watching. Such peeping toms, like exhibitionists, don't want any further sexual contact with the women they spy on. Most voyeurs are shy and have had trouble making friends with women. If you like looking at naked people or pictures of them, that doesn't make you a voyeur; the diagnosis of voyeurism is made only when the person spied on is unsuspecting, when the peeping is repetitive, and when it is a main source of sexual satisfaction.

Perversions—II
Whips and Chains

Most of the paraphilias are found exclusively or primarily among men. But two of the best known—sadism and masochism—are relatively common in women, too. The garden variety of S&M involves sexual fantasies such as being raped or bedroom bondage games of the sort described in *The Joy of Sex*. The psychiatrist's manual regards this level of S&M as harmless.

To qualify for the diagnosis "sexual masochism," a person must have persistent and intense fantasies of being turned on through suffering, and have acted them out in such a way as to have risked physical harm. People who exclusively prefer sexual scenarios where they are humiliated, bound, or otherwise made to suffer also qualify for the diagnosis. Although masochistic fantasies are common among women, men are more likely to act them out.

Every masochist, of course, longs to find an obliging sadist. Mutually consenting sadists and masochists can form relationships that stay stable for years. Sadistic fantasies such as torturing someone are probably about as common as masochistic ones. But the diagnosis "sexual sadism" is reserved for those who actually act out such fantasies. An occasional foray into sadism during foreplay with a consenting partner is considered in the realm of normality, not perversion. But people who need to inflict physical or mental suffering on someone to become sexually aroused are, clinically speaking, sadists. In the extreme (and very rare) range fall brutal rapists and those who murder for lust.

How to Tell a Schizophrenic

If you suspect someone is really crazy—that is, schizophrenic—the following checklist from the new diagnostic manual for psychiatrists will help you decide. A schizophrenic must display at least one symptom from any of the following categories:

1. Delusions
   ☐ delusions of being controlled, for example, through thoughts broadcast on TV

☐ other bizarre delusions (providing the person is not also depressed or highly excited, in which case the diagnosis would be different)
☐ delusions that are "somatic, grandiose, religious, or nihilistic" in content
☐ any delusion that includes a hallucination
☐ preoccupation with a delusion or hallucination

2. Hallucinations
☐ auditory hallucinations, such as a voice making a running commentary on the person's activities, or two voices in conversation, or a voice occasionally speaking a few words
☐ any sort of hallucination that lasts throughout the day, for several days at a time, or intermittently for a month

3. Disordered thoughts
☐ disorganized thinking, if accompanied by inappropriate expression of feelings, delusions, hallucinations, or other strange behavior

These signs must last for at least two weeks after a noticeable change in the person's usual behavior. They must not be due to any physical cause.

Why Schizophrenics Talk Strangely

"Now to eat if one cannot the other can—and if we can't the girseau O. C. Washpots prizebloom capacities'. . . ." These lines are not from Joyce's *Ulysses* but rather are examples of the speech of schizophrenic patients. Though schizophrenics don't speak this way all the time, the confused and confusing patterns of such speech are so typical of the disorder that psychiatrists can easily pick out "schizophrenic language."

A study of samples of schizophrenic writing shows why it is so garbled. While it typically starts out making sense, by the time a sentence is finished, it is likely to be completely sidetracked. It seems schizophrenics are unable to ignore interfering associations with words. When ideas associated with a word in the sentence pop into their head, rather than ignoring them (as we do during normal speech), they express them. As association follows association, the sentence becomes completely confusing. For example, the author of the passage about O. C. Washpots continues, "O. C. Washpots under-atterned against—bred to pattern. Animal sequestration capacities and animal sequestered capacities under leash—and animal secretions. . . ."

Schizophrenics are particularly susceptible to such thought intrusions because the disorder itself is characterized by disrupted attention. Schizophrenics typically are highly distractible; they have great difficulty focusing on tasks that require close attention. The ability to focus attention is essential to completing a sentence properly—as we find out when we are exhausted, upset, or drunk. If we don't tune out verbal static, then associations will invade the ~~county~~ sentence we're in the middle of ~~typing typing piping~~ speaking.

Are People Crazy Who Kill Themselves?

You'd have to be crazy, you might think, to take your own life. But although most people who try to kill themselves are indeed depressed and upset, only a small portion are truly psychotic, or "crazy" in the sense of being out of touch with reality.

Schizophrenics, who are by definition "out of touch with reality," have a very low incidence of suicide compared to people with other kinds of mental illness. Depressed people have the highest rate of suicide: three times the rate for schizophrenics and six times the rate for garden-variety neurotics. After interviewing relatives of people who had killed themselves, researchers concluded that only about 5 to 20 percent may have been psychotic—completely out of touch with reality—at the time of their death.

Though suicidal people may not be totally out of touch with reality, evidence nevertheless suggests that their patterns of thinking are somewhat distorted. Suicide victims tend to be rigid and to

see things in black and white. This rigid, either-or thinking seems to lead them to conclude that they have no choice but to take their life: they are too inflexible to consider alternative solutions to their problems. Suicide notes reveal another curious twist of thought. The notes often show that the writers are looking forward to the attention they will gain by killing themselves. They seem to forget they won't be around to enjoy it.

Who Commits Suicide?

At some point in their lives, between 2 and 5 percent of Americans will try to kill themselves. Only about one out of eight attempted suicides succeeds, but one in ten of those who make unsuccessful attempts will later succeed. The going clinical wisdom is that, by and large, people who make unsuccessful attempts are vying for attention. Those who succeed are deadly serious.

Men outnumber women three to one among successful suicide attempts. Among unsuccessful tries, the ratio reverses: women outnumber men by about the same ratio. However, the gap between the sexes has been closing over the years.

The suicide rate among blacks has for years been about one-third that for whites. Recently, though, the rates have been more even, due to a striking rise in suicides among younger blacks. By the late 1970s the rates for blacks and whites had become just about the same up to age forty. After age forty the old pattern prevails, with older blacks much less likely to commit suicide than older whites.

The older one gets, the higher the risk. Among white males, a seventy-year-old is six times more likely to commit suicide than is a twenty-year-old. Changes late in life make people more prone to suicide: retirement, children's departure from the home, menopause, death of a spouse.

Family lessens the risk. Married people with children have low suicide rates; among the unmarried, the always single have lower rates than the divorced. The chances of any given person's suicide, though, are highly remote: the suicide rates even of "high-risk" groups are reckoned in terms of a few hundred in every 100,000 people.

Who, then, are these "high risk" groups?

☐ The seriously depressed. However, though several million people become seriously depressed each year, very few go on to commit suicide.
☐ People who are "in their right mind." People who commit suicide usually are rational and in touch with reality when they do so.
☐ People with terminal diseases. Being aware one will die soon does not make suicide less likely. Indeed, many terminally ill people take their lives to avoid pain or shorten the suffering of loved ones.
☐ People who threaten suicide. Although most threats are empty, the rate of suicide victims who have let others know their intent is almost three out of four.

But:

☐ People with obvious reasons to take their lives often don't. The reason one person commits suicide while another who suffers the same stress (for example, death of a spouse) does not still puzzles experts.
☐ Relatives of those who commit suicide are no more nor less likely to commit suicide themselves.
☐ San Francisco does not have the highest suicide rate in America. As of 1980, Las Vegas, Nevada, was Number One. Its suicide rate was 30.5 per 100,000; the national average was just 12 per 100,000.

Suicide: Second Thoughts

What is it like to almost die by your own hand? Do these who attempt suicide go through a different sort of experience from others who have a scrape with death?

While data are scant, since near-victims of suicide are hard to find, evidence suggests they experience almost-dying much like anyone else. For example, eight people who miraculously survived near-death experiences, recalled a series of events as they were "dying" that typically included seeing their own body from afar, floating through a dark space or tunnel, seeing a golden light, sensing a "presence," and so on (see "What Is It Like to Die?").

But there is one significant difference. All those who had nearly died by their own hand but survived reported that, as a result of their near-death experience, they would never consider suicide again. Given that many people who kill themselves have made previous attempts, clearly not all experience this change of heart. It would seem that the moments at the actual brink of death were transformatory. One cure for suicidal tendencies, then would seem to be almost succeeding.

Criminals and Psychopaths

People are often called psychopaths, but we make a sharp distinction between criminal behavior and behavior we consider truly psychopathic. Psychopaths act antisocially throughout life, often for no good reason, and seem to suffer no feelings of guilt or remorse for what they have done. They may steal, lie, and even kill as casually as most of us would take a bath. They do what they feel like, disregarding all moral values and the rights and welfare of others. Yet, perhaps surprisingly, most criminals are not psychopaths and indeed psychopaths are responsible for only a tiny fraction of crimes committed.

Psychopaths are unusual people. Not only do they seem to feel no guilt, but they also do not usually feel the other emotions with which we are familiar. In terrifying situations, they may be calm; threatened by a charging lion, they are cool; nausea, fear, disgust, affection, and love are foreign to them. In a sense they are less than human because they do not share human emotions. But in another sense they have an advantage over normal people because they are not hampered by concerns about their own safety or feelings for other people, emotions that interfere with action.

In contrast, criminals usually do have normal feelings of fear, love, disgust, and so on though they do have different codes of ethics and perhaps different reactions to situations. They do react; they are afraid when threatened; they do care for their loved ones; and they usually have clear rules of behavior that they stick to. But these rules are different from ours—they are criminal rules. For example, a criminal may see nothing wrong with killing a rival or stealing from a big store, but would be as upset as anyone at lying to a friend. Thus criminals are in many ways quite similar to anyone else except that they commit crimes, whereas psychopaths are very strange and almost not social beings. The best advice is to stay away from both of them.

Position Available: Ex-Con Preferred

Whom would you trust more: an ex-convict or a former mental patient?

The greater stigma seems to be attached to the former mental patient. For example, a group of college students were given thirty situations in which they had to choose between an ex-con and an ex-patient. Some of the more telling results:

☐ Most of the men said that if they had to be one or the other, they'd rather be an ex-con than a former mental patient.
☐ Prospective mothers thought it more prudent to entrust their children to the care of an ex-con.
☐ Former convicts were thought to be more trustworthy in an emergency.
☐ A permanent job with high responsibility was seen as more wisely given to the ex-con, although the former patient would be the choice for a job with minor responsibility.

The preference for the ex-convict over the ex-patient prevailed even though the people responding admitted they had never had any negative experiences with former mental patients.

What You Should Know about Your Therapist

There is no *Consumer Reports* rating sheet of therapists. Some are very good, some are not so good; the patient, finally, must be the judge of the effectiveness of his or her therapy. There have been literally hundreds of studies of the effectiveness of therapy, but no firm conclusions that therapy is always helpful—indeed, there is some evidence that therapy can sometimes cause setbacks.

In general, the evidence shows the following:

☐ The outcome of therapy is not related to the specific methods or outlook of the therapist. A behavior therapist, psychoanalyst, or family therapist could all have the same luck—or lack of it—with a given patient.

☐ Seasoned therapists do better than novices. What's more, experienced therapists tend to be more like each other in how they do therapy, regardless of their orientation, than they are like others who might share their outlook.

☐ Paraprofessionals (nurses, hospital aides, even volunteers) often do therapy as well as therapists who have been formally trained.

☐ Having been through therapy does not seem to make a therapist more effective, nor does having gone through a formal training program. Training in specific skills and techniques (such as communications) does, however, improve a therapist's abilities.

The most telling assets of a therapist are matters of personal style, not the type of therapy or training. The best therapists share three traits: (1) accurate empathy, or being able to understand the patient by stepping into the patient's shoes; (2) warmth, or being able to like a patient; and (3) genuineness, or simply being sincere

in dealing with a patient. In short, in shopping for a therapist these are probably the attributes to scout for: empathy, warmth, and genuineness. And, most of all, experience.

The YAVIS

The overwhelming majority of people who seek help from therapists are not necessarily the people who need it most. Studies show that the bulk of the patients of private therapists share certain traits: in the words of one researcher, they are "youthful, attractive, verbal, intelligent, and successful"—YAVIS, for short.

Why should such people go into therapy at all? They see therapy as meaningful and helpful, a way to learn more about themselves. Ironically, these people tend not to be seriously impaired by psychological problems. The severely distressed in society, who are not able to function in daily life, are far less likely to get the quality of psychotherapy the YAVIS enjoy. Instead, they often end up in hospital psychiatric wards or assembly-line outpatient clinics, where they are more likely to get medication than therapy.

Psychotherapy, A to Z

Psychotherapy is a child of the twentieth century. Freud's original concepts of what therapy should be came into vogue in the early years of this century, and now, more than three-quarters of a century later, there are hundreds of competing versions. Here are some of the more exotic and unique therapy techniques to arrive in the mental-health marketplace:

☐ **Anti-expectation psychotherapy. The therapist contradicts the patient's expectations; for example, the therapist might encourage the patient to amplify symptoms.**
☐ **Bibliotherapy. Patients read selected books.**

☐ Computer therapy. The therapist is a computer.
☐ Cooking therapy. Patients channel their anxieties, tensions, and aggressions by cutting, chopping, and beating meat and vegetables.
☐ Dance therapy. Therapy is through movement rather than words.
☐ Exaggeration therapy. The therapist invents increasingly dramatic versions of the patient's complaint until the patient smiles or laughs at himself or herself.
☐ Flooding. A phobic patient is confronted with the thing or situation feared most, which floods the patient with anxiety and distress.
☐ Horticultural therapy. Therapist and patient garden together.
☐ Mirror-image therapy. The patient gazes at his or her face in a mirror and free associates.
☐ Past-lives therapy. The patient is hypnotized and relives "past lives" to understand what's going wrong with this one.
☐ Soap-opera therapy. soap opera buffs use the goings-on in their favorite show as a way to address their own melodramas.
☐ Zaralaya psychoenergetic technique. Patients get in touch with "the flow of psychic energy within and between people."

Health
and
Happiness

After mental disorders, we would like to end the book on a more positive note. Psychologists are primarily interested in healthy, well-functioning people. It is appropriate that psychologists have concentrated on trying to discover what leads to a healthy life, a full life, and a happy life. Although we do not have the final answers—sadly, we cannot give you a five-step plan to guarantee happiness— we have found out something about this mysterious quality, and that is what this section deals with.

Throughout this section, keep in mind that people are very different. What makes one person happy may be unimportant to another; what upsets one may pass by another as if it never happened. But the research here is based on studies of a great many people, so that even though it does not provide final answers, it may provide some hints or clues that will apply to you.

The Road to Happiness

Unfortunately, psychologists do not know precisely what brings happiness. There is little question that different factors are essential for different people, and the exact mixture that leads to happiness may also be different at different times in life. However, various studies of happiness have provided some tentative answers and some surprises.

Almost everyone says that love, and long-term romantic relationships, are essential for happiness. People who are in such relationships are almost always happier than those who are not.

Sex is considerably less important than love for most people. A good sex life helps, but it neither guarantees happiness nor is absolutely necessary for it. Some people with great sex lives are very unhappy; some with poor sex lives are happy.

And the type of sex does not seem to matter very much either, within limits. Homosexuals (male or female) say that they are just as happy as heterosexuals. However, those with mixed sexual preferences—partly homosexual, partly heterosexual (the so-called bisexuals)—say they are the least happy. You might have thought that bisexuality was the best of both worlds, and maybe it is in some ways, but these people don't seem to experience as much happiness as those with one preference or the other.

Married people (and those living together for some time) are happier than single people. This is especially true for women, and most true for older women. Apparently, in our society, despite some changes, life is still very difficult for an older woman who is single. The old double standard is alive.

Careers and occupations are also very important to happiness. Most people seem to want something to do, and to feel that what they are doing is worthwhile. These days, moreover, it seems that taking care of the home and the children is not sufficient for many people. Although some married women are quite happy as housewives, many are not. In fact, married women who have regular jobs tend to be happier than those who do not.

And then there is money. Perhaps the most surprising result of the work on happiness is that money is less important than most of us would have thought. At the very low end of the economic ladder, money is critical. People who are at or below the poverty level are much less happy than those who have more money. But once above this level, the amount of money people have has little effect on their happiness. The rich are not happier than the middle class; the middle class are not happier than the somewhat poorer working class. It's an old saying that money doesn't buy happiness and, for once, the old saying seems to be true.

In Sickness and in Health

Each year, every man, woman, and child has an average of about two episodes of illness or injury that demand medical attention or staying at home. On any given day, about one person in thirty has such a problem.

Each year the average American has close to twenty days where normal activities are simply restricted because of illness or injury; on any given day one person in seven is taking it easy. Young people have fewer such days; for those under twenty-five, the average is around eleven per year. For those between forty-five and sixty-five, the average is over twenty-five sick days per year; the sixty-five-and-over crowd collects about forty sick days yearly.

The common cold, of course, is the most frequent reason: one in every five sick days is from a cold.

Fats and Thins

It seems as if just about everyone in the country is on a diet. We all want to be tall and thin, and since we can't do anything about our height, we concentrate on our weight. But, alas some people find that it is not so easy to lose weight. There are those who gain a few pounds on a vacation and can lose the weight in a week by skipping dessert or taking smaller portions; others who have been overweight for years go on strenuous, backbreaking diets for months, lose a pound or two, and then gain it right back over a weekend. It isn't fair.

The basic principle is supposed to be that if you reduce your calories and exercise as much as usual, you will eventually lose weight. Obviously, if what goes in is less than what you burn up, weight must go down. True. The problem is that some people, to lose any weight at all, must practically starve themselves. The suffering is so great, so continuous, and in the long run so destructive that they go off the diet and back on goes the weight. Why is it so hard for some and so easy for others?

The answer seems to be that some people are, in a sense, born to be fat. Just as some of us are born to be tall (that is, our heredity makes us tall), others are born to be heavier than others. Not everyone is built like a *Vogue* model (thank God). Some are stockier than others, some muscular, some just plain bigger. If you were a little shorter than you wanted to be, you might be sorry but you would accept it. But if you are a little heavier than the world (or your friend) would like you to be, you fight like crazy to lose weight. And this doesn't work very well, because nature—your genes, or your basic, natural body—has decreed that you will not be skinny, but will be rounded or even a little heavy. And you can't fool with Mother Nature. Yes, you can lose weight, but your body naturally returns to its right weight whenever it gets a chance. If you continue dieting all your life, you may stay thin. But once you go off the diet, rather than remaining thin, your body jumps right back to its original and natural shape.

This does not mean that you should be very fat. As far as we know, no one (unless they suffer from a specific physical disorder) should be grossly overweight. But it does mean that 5 or 10 percent overweight may be your lot in life. Trying to lose that weight will take enormous efforts, and may not be healthy.

Sugar on the Brain

Some years back a disorder called "hypoglycemia" became a popular self-diagnosis. Hypoglycemia is a condition typified by depression, anxiety, irritability, and lethargy, all brought on when people whose bodies don't metabolize sugar properly eat sweet foods. The clinical test for establishing the diagnosis of hypoglycemia is a fast, followed by drinking a measured dose of a glucose concoction; for the next several hours, blood glucose levels are monitored. If they fall too low, the diagnosis of hypoglycemia is confirmed.

Following a spate of popular books on the topic, hundreds of thousands of people who suspected they suffered from the disorder flocked to doctors for the glucose test. So many of these would-be hypoglycemics failed to get low enough readings on the glucose test that physicans began to suspect their symptoms were psychological, not metabolic, in origin. Hypoglycemia was labeled a "fad disorder" in prestigious medical journals; physicians were warned to be wary of patients who had diagnosed themselves as hypoglycemics—"hypochondriacs" was thought to be more like it.

Then on the scene came a group of researchers who took a new look at the problem. They collected patients who had the psychological signs of hypoglycemia but did not seem to have low glucose levels. The researchers did a new sort of test: they monitored the patients' brain waves during the glucose test at the same time as they measured blood glucose levels. The results: when people reported the worst psychological symptoms—intense anxiety, crying, and so on—their brain waves showed irregular patterns, much like those seen during epileptic seizures. But their glucose levels did not indicate an abnormality. Further tests, though, revealed that the abnormal brain waves occurred while their blood *insulin* levels were high. The body's metabolism of sugar can result in either sort of irregularity—abnormal levels of insulin or of glucose. The physicians had been testing only for glucose, and so missed making a diagnosis when insulin was the culprit. The patients were redeemed—they weren't hypochondriacs, but sufferers from hyperinsulinism.

The Sugar Eaters

Sugar does us no good either nutritionally (its high calories offer no vitamins or proteins) or, quite possibly, mentally (see "Sugar on the Brain"). Yet Americans consume an average 128 pounds of the sweet stuff each year. Sugar is hard to avoid—it's an ingredient in such unlikely foods as tomato sauce, salad dressing, and chili, to name a few.

Who eats the most sugar? Taking the 128 pounds per year as the standard of 100 percent for sugar consumption:

Children 3-5 years consume	120 pounds
Children 6-8 years consume	141 pounds
Girls 9-11 consume	148 pounds
Boys 9-11 consume	163 pounds
Girls 12-19 consume	148 pounds
Boys 12-19 consume	187 pounds
Women 20-34 consume	125 pounds
Men 20-34 consume	159 pounds
Women over 35 consume	97 pounds
Men over 35 consume	141 pounds

The Hidden Costs of Rush Hour

For those of you who commute to work daily, it will come as no surprise that researchers have confirmed that commuting is tough.

Commuters of three types were compared: those who had an easy commute, driving less than eight miles between home and work or with less than thirteen minutes travel time; those with a medium commute of up to fourteen miles and a time of twenty minutes; and those with a hard one, up to fifty miles and seventy-five minutes. As you might expect, the longer the commute, the worse the wear and tear. Long commuters had higher blood pressure, complained more, did more poorly on performance tests given when they got to work, and arrived in a worse mood. What's more, the longer they had been commuting that distance, the higher their blood pressure.

Type A Behavior and Heart Attacks

By now everyone knows that smoking increases the chances of getting a heart attack, that being very overweight is also bad for your health, and that eating too much fat isn't so great either. But the latest idea is that our personalities play an important role in increasing the risk of heart trouble. In particular, there may be certain types of people, called type A people, who are more likely to have heart attacks than other people, who are called type B.

Type A people are always on the go, rush around, work to deadlines, worry if there is a delay, worry about work and life, and have trouble relaxing. They are not calm, not easygoing, not, in the terms of the sixties, "laid back." If things are slow at work, instead of enjoying the leisure, type A people are concerned that

nothing is getting done, that business must be bad, that they are wasting time. Even vacations are a whirlwind of activity, seeing all the sights, or swimming miles every day, or playing twenty sets of competitive tennis—none of this sunbathing and a gentle soak in the pool for our type A's.

The Type A habits include the following:

☐ speedy, explosive speech when there is no need to rush
☐ eating and walking fast
☐ becoming impatient whenever people or events take too long
☐ always trying to do several things at once, such as dictating while driving

☐ steering conversations to topics of general interest, and only feigning interest in anything else
☐ feeling guilty over spare time spent taking things easy
☐ not noticing things of beauty or worth beyond a narrow focus of interest
☐ judging people in terms of numbers, such as salary, grades earned, or articles published
☐ chronic feelings of urgency, plus the habit of scheduling more things in less time
☐ tense, nervous gestures or tics
☐ the personal credo that success comes from doing things more quickly than anyone else
☐ an aggressive, competitive, and hostile stance toward others—especially rival Type A's

Type B's, as you might guess, have none of the habits that typify the A's. For example, they rarely feel rushed or impatient, and they don't get hostile or competitive. They can relax and have fun without feeling guilty, and work without being panicked and agitated.

Sometimes a job can define a type. For example, positions that involve constant deadlines, high levels of competition, and drive, require type A behavior. Therefore people in type A jobs tend to act like type A people, even if their own personalities are not really that type. Because these jobs demand certain behavior, staying in them requires appropriate behavior.

Both type A personalities and type A jobs increase the chance of heart attacks. The stresses produced by this kind of activity take a toll on the person's physical condition and strain the heart so that it is weaker. Although not all A people have heart attacks, and not all type B people escape them, the former have a higher risk of a heart attack because of their personalities. Research on type A behavior is still new and most psychologists and physicians are not fully convinced that *this* particular personality type has such harmful effects; nevertheless, there is general agreement that personality does play a role in health and probably in heart trouble.

Changing one's behavior can possibly help prevent heart attacks or improve the chances of recovery if you have already had one. Indeed, many clinics now give heart patients instruction and therapy based on teaching them to behave in a more relaxed, calmer, "type B" manner. The old advice to take it easy is now being taught in formal, serious programs designed to help victims of heart attacks. Whether it will prove effective is uncertain. We do know that it is difficult to change your style of life all of a sudden, heart attack or not, but it may be that such a change is essential for recovery. It is probably helpful in avoiding attacks in the first place.

Aging and Senility

One of our greatest fears concerning getting old is that we will become senile. It is true that some elderly people do suffer from serious deterioration of their mental abilities, to the extent that they are unable to remember much, cannot think clearly, and generally cannot take care of themselves. However, careful research by psychologists and others has produced some really good news—senility is not a typical effect of aging. Few people become senile no matter how long they live. In fact, senility seems to be due to a specific disease and only 10 or 15 percent of people ever suffer from that disease.

The condition that leads to senility is called Alzheimer's disease. It consists of severe breakdown of certain kinds of cells in the brain and is quite distinct. Everyone's brain loses some cells as it gets older, and there is some deterioration of nerve cells. But for most people, these effects are minor and have little or no effect on mental abilities. Only those who have Alzheimer's disease or who have specific physical conditions such as strokes become senile. In other words, there is no reason why most people cannot remain just as smart and sharp as ever when they get older. Senility is a terrible condition, but it strikes only the unlucky few.

Age and Memory

Have you ever forgotten a name and said "I must be getting old"? Most of us assume that as we get older our minds will become less sharp and in particular that we will start forgetting names and words. Whatever else old age will bring, we assume that it will affect our memories. Once again we have good news—age has much less effect on memory than is usually thought.

Research done over the past ten years has shown that elderly people's memories differ little if at all from those of younger people. As long as they are not suffering from a condition such as Alzheimer's disease (senility), mental abilities (see "Aging and Senility"), elderly people are just about as sharp as they ever were. They do react less quickly than younger people, and therefore are slower in doing intellectual tasks, including remembering. But if time is not crucial, under most circumstances old people remember just fine.

Then why, you may ask, does it seem as if old people have more difficulty remembering names and other trivia than younger people do? One reason may be that even though they make no more mistakes than they did when they were younger, whenever they make a mistake they blame their age. They say, "I'm getting old and my memory is going." When younger people say this, they don't really mean it. When older people say it, they believe it. Thus every time they forget a name, they convince themselves that it is because their minds are going. Not true. They may have some trouble with certain kinds of tasks, but generally age has little effect on memory or any other kind of mental ability. Cheer up—getting old may not be as bad as we think (see "Age and Happiness").

Smoking Is an Addiction

Everyone knows how hard it is for most people to stop smoking. The typical reaction by nonsmokers is that smokers are weak or self-indulgent or just plain stupid. After all, if you know that something is bad for you, why not just give it up? Yet recent research indicats that the difficulty in stopping is not due to any weakness in the brain or personality, but is actually caused by a real physical addiction.

If someone is hooked on morphine, we sympathize because we know it is hard to break an addiction. Well, nicotine also causes an addiction, and it may be even worse than the addiction to morphine. When smokers go cold turkey (stop all at once), they typically have physical reactions such as sweating, bleeding gums, and other unpleasant indications of addiction. Also, there is evidence that people smoke just enough to maintain the "right" amount of nicotine in their system. They "need" their fix, and they smoke until they get the desired amount.

One important implication of this is that low-nicotine cigarettes may not be such a good idea. Addicted smokers may switch to the low-nicotine brands, but they still need the same amount of nicotine. So what many of them do is simply smoke more cigarettes, or smoke them longer and inhale more. That way they get what they need in terms of nicotine, the tobacco companies sell even more cigarettes, and everyone's happy. Unfortunately, this does not reduce the amount of nicotine the smokers get, so their health suffers just as much. And they probably get even more tar, which is also bad for them. The tobacco companies hate this research, but for the moment, it seems to be accurate.

The Myth of the "Heroin Overdose"

Newspaper headlines frequently trumpet reports of heroin addicts dying from an "overdose"; rock star Janis Joplin supposedly was a victim. But in fact such overdoses are far less frequent than they might seem. A body of evidence points to the good possibility that most of the deaths attributed to an overdose are due to other causes entirely.

For one thing, dying of a morphine or heroin overdose takes up to twelve hours. During that time lethargy and stupor are followed by coma; when death results, it is from respiratory failure. At any point during this period an injection of a narcotic antagonist called "nalorphine" will reverse the whole process in minutes—and nalorphine is stocked in every hospital emergency room.

For another, the amount of morphine or heroin it would take to kill an addict is immense—up to fifty times the standard dose. Addicts develop an increasing physical tolerance to the drugs, and there are recorded cases where doses this massive did not result in a single medically significant change—not even drowsiness. In short, addicts are remarkably resistant to overdose.

An additional fact—the standard procedures coroners use to conclude that a death was due to overdose do not actually verify that conclusion. The coroner's phrase "death from heroin overdose" actually means simply that the person died after injecting heroin and that there is no other known cause, such as suicide, violence, or infection. Coroners rarely, if ever, bother to perform the laboratory analyses that are needed to firmly establish the precise quantity of the drug present in the body.

Most deaths labeled "overdose" have a clinical picture quite different from a true overdose death. Instead of taking several hours, these deaths occur within a few minutes of injection, sometimes so rapidly that the syringe is still found in the dead person's vein. Along with the rapid onset of death, there is frequently pulmonary edema, the filling of the lungs with fluid. Indeed, careful studies of such deaths have ruled out a reaction to heroin per se as the cause—typically, the victim has used a standard, unadulterated dose.

What, then, is the cause of mislabeled deaths from overdose? Heroin is sometimes adulterated with poisons such as strychnine. Another likely cause is a cross-tolerance reaction, the result of taking two drugs at the same time that don't mix well. Central nervous system depressants, like alcohol and barbiturates, are the prime candidates. To set the record straight, Janis Joplin had been drinking just before she took her fatal injection of heroin.

Index